Business English Activities

Flexible Lesson Plans with Worksheets

by
Sally Beetham Tilley
Justin Adair

Ernst Klett Verlag für Wissen und Bildung
Stuttgart · Dresden

Business English Activities
Flexible Lesson Plans with Worksheets

by
Sally Beetham Tilley
Justin Adair

Gedruckt auf Recyclingpapier, hergestellt aus 100 % Altpapier.

1. Auflage 1 4 3 2 1 | 1997 96 95 94

Alle Drucke dieser Auflage können im Unterricht nebeneinander benutzt werden, sie sind untereinander unverändert.
Die letzte Zahl bezeichnet das Jahr dieses Druckes.

Redaktion: David Shallis
Zeichnung: Roman Lang
Umschlagsgestaltung: Hanjo Schmidt
Druck: Süddeutscher Zeitungsdienst, Aalen.

Printed in Germany.
ISBN 3-12-537930-X

Contents

Introduction

Who this book is for?

Many of us find that we are expected to teach Business English courses with no business background of our own and only a general English training to fall back on. Understandably, we worry about being able to produce whatever it is our learners need. If you are in this position, then this book is for you.

Business English Activities was written to help **general English teachers** adapt their existing language knowledge and teaching techniques to Business English courses. Reading through the activities and trying them out with classes should help develop a clearer idea of what it is business learners actually do and what their language needs are.

Business English Activities will also be useful to **experienced teachers of Business English** looking for different ways of introducing and extending language and enabling learners to carry out particular business-related tasks.

Although the activities in this book were designed with in-service learners in mind, most of them can also be used with trainees and business students as they stand, or with different subject matter.

General Business English

To many people, Business English suggests specialized fields such as merchant banking, marine insurance or mechanical engineering, each with its own obscure jargon and procedures. Some teachers do in fact specialize in these fields and become familiar with their distinctive features. This is the area of EFL known as 'English for Specific Purposes' or ESP.

For the majority of business learners, however, the jargon of their particular speciality is easily acquired and not really the problem. What they do need is help to bind that jargon together into meaningful communication in the broader business context: taking care of visitors, talking about a product range, describing a procedure or taking part in a meeting.

The language of such activities is **common to all businesses** and can be thought of as 'General Business English'. This includes a substantial body of vocabulary. For instance, all companies need *management* and *premises*; they *plan, negotiate contracts, advertise, invoice* and *make a profit* or *loss*; *staff* are *employed* and *trained, work* in *plants* or *offices*, use *equipment*, attend *meetings*, interpret *diagrams* and read *reports*.

The General Business English teacher

Most Business English teachers find themselves working with learners from a range of different industries and businesses. Many companies are of course themselves made up of 'colonies' of specialists who may not know very much about each others' work. Bank staff, for instance, may serve at the counter, but they could just as well be corporate loan experts, currency traders or dealers in government bonds.

Clearly, we cannot be expected to have an in-depth understanding of all fields of business activity, nor do we need to pretend that we have. Bankers do not, after all, go to language courses to learn about their own business. The teacher's role here is often less one of teaching in the conventional sense than of facilitating, of enabling learners to say **what they want to say** in the target language. In order to do this effectively, we need to develop a grasp of **general business practice**. The best way to acquire such knowledge is obviously to talk to practising business people – in other words, our learners – who are usually only too happy to explain the principles and procedures involved. If you feel apprehensive about doing this, you will find that using the activities in this book makes it easy for both sides; and as your understanding of the general workings of business increases, you will also build up a more detailed picture of the companies you actually work with.

Keep up to date with business trends by following developments in the media and keeping an eye on the specialist press, such as the business section of 'The European' newspaper, 'The Financial Times', 'The Wall Street Journal' and 'The Economist' magazine.

Motivating the business learner

Some business learners - especially managers - only find time to learn or brush up their language shortly before a foreign trip, when they may also be preparing for negotiations, making arrangements for their families and being innoculated against tropical diseases! Even learners who are not under this sort of pressure usually have to take their language lessons at less than ideal times, such as early in the morning or at the end of the working day. Motivation is essential if regular attendance and full concentration are to be ensured in conditions like these.

Business people, like any other adults, rarely go anywhere or do anything without knowing why and what is expected of them. Managers, in particular, are used to taking the initiative and being more or less responsible for what happens around them. And yet teachers often limit their business learners to passive, receptive roles, ignoring the experience and expertise they have to offer.

It is now widely recognised that learners are more motivated and learn more efficiently if they are actively **involved**, if they are able to bring their experience and expertise into the language classroom. A successful Business English course is also likely to be one in which learners are encouraged to take the initiative in language learning, trying to communicate even if they make some errors along the way, finding a way around gaps in their vocabulary and recording new language so that it is memorable and accessible.

The activities in this book demand just this sort of approach from learners, and help them develop the techniques they need to continue **to learn for themselves outside the classroom**.

The activities

All the activities in this book can be used **in any order** and at a range of **different levels**. In general, they were designed with weekly 90-minute lessons in mind but can be integrated into any other teaching timetable as required. The activities in Section A, however, will take less time. Some others, particularly in Section D, may need to be spread over two or more weekly lessons, depending on the size of the class. All the activities can be used with learners from **any business**.

Many of the activities can be **reused with different topics**. You will probably want to try them out in the form described here first of all and then adapt them to the needs of particular classes. The worksheets at the back of the book can be photocopied and handed out to learners. In some cases, you may prefer to copy the worksheets onto the board or flipchart, or show them on an overhead projector (OHP) if one is available.

The language

Each activity includes an overview of the language items that lower-level learners are likely to need in order to take part effectively. You may want to replace or modify the language items suggested to suit the needs of your particular learners.

Vocabulary Where an activity depends on a specific set of vocabulary, this is given or indicated in the **Language** overview for that activity. Learners will often also want to use the jargon of their particular industry or profession. As explained above, this ESP vocabulary is rarely a real problem for the teacher as learners normally either know it or can get hold of the expressions they need without difficulty. Where this is not the case, they should:

- ask other members of the class;
- find out whether their company has a glossary (usually available from the personnel department or translation section);
- look at company publications in English, such as brochures and reports.

Grammar This book does not set out to teach grammar as such, although grammatical structures of various kinds occur in the language overviews of some of the activities. In general, the approach here is to focus only on those structures that learners need to carry out an activity as described.

Functions Several of the activities in this book focus principally on functional language. In these cases, lower-level learners may need more practice of the form before they go on to the **Production** phase of the activity. With more advanced classes, you will probably want to take the exponents listed in the language overview as a starting point and elicit further and / or more sophisticated versions.

Pronunciation Although the activity teaching notes make no specific mention of pronunciation, sound, stress and intonation should of course be checked and practised as necessary before learners begin with freer practice.

Presenting information

In a number of the activities, learners are asked to present information to the rest of their class. At lower levels this can be done by reading out a set of straightforward statements or a simple text. Higher-level learners can be asked to give formal presentations (see **D2: Structuring a presentation**).

Whatever the level, presentations will normally be more successful if the audience has a task to perform while they are listening, such as noting down the most important fact(s) they hear, recording the main information in the form of a diagram or preparing one or two questions for the speaker. More advanced learners could use discussion tasks as opportunities to practise business meetings language (see **D4: Taking part in meetings**).

British and American English

The language of these activities is essentially international English; that is, neither especially British nor American but acceptable and comprehensible to both, as well as to the many non-native speakers who use English as a business *lingua franca*. Activity B3, however, is in British letter-style.

THE ACTIVITIES

THE ACTIVITIES
THE ACTIVITIES

Section A
Business Vocabulary

1. **Mind maps**
2. **Word families**
3. **Word partnerships**
4. **Starter phrases**
5. **Testing vocabulary**

A solid working vocabulary is a high priority for most learners of Business English. This section demonstrates several different ways in which business vocabulary can be presented and extended.

It also shows some ways in which new expressions can be organized and stored. Encourage learners to try them all out and choose the ones that suit them best.

Mind maps

Learners are sometimes unaware of how much vocabulary they already have. Conversely, they may only find out that they are missing important expressions when they actually need to use them in their work.

This activity shows how the vocabulary of a particular subject area can be identified and extended.

Preparation

Level

Intermediate to advanced

Language

Lexical sets (see Worksheets A1.1 and A1.2 for examples)

Before the lesson

Look at Worksheets A1.1 and A1.2 and list one or two other words your learners could mind-map.

You will need

- one copy of Worksheet A1.1 (or A1.2) per learner;
- dictionaries.

The Activity

Introduction

Warm up by writing the word *company* (or *product*) in the middle of the board. Ask learners to call out one word each that they associate with the word on the board. List them on the side of the board.

Development

1. Hand out one copy of Worksheet A1.1 (or A1.2) to each person in the class. Give them a few minutes to look at the mind map and memorize as much of it as they can.
2. Learners turn over their worksheets. Working in small groups, they write down as many words as they can remember.
3. Ask each group in turn to reconstruct a section of the mind map on the board. When no one can come up with any more of the words, ask them to compare their work with the original.

Production

1. Still in groups, learners try to add to the mind map on the board, using dictionaries if necessary. Any words on the side of the board that are not already in the map can be included at this point. Some words may of course occur more than once, in different connections.
2. Level and time permitting, you could now give the class a new word around which to build a mind map. Note that there is no 'correct' way of making a mind map; it all depends on your mind!

Further ideas

- Draw up a mind map and then blank out the initial word and / or the 'connector' words at the centre of clusters (e.g. *organization, history* or *management* on Worksheet A1.1). Learners have to work out what they were.

- Make a copy of a mind map and blank out a number of the words. Learners work alone or in groups to complete the map. Low-level learners could be given the missing words in a separate list.
- Make two copies of a mind map and blank out a number of different words on each. Learners work in pairs, each with one of the sheets, telling their partners what they think the missing words could be. Partners confirm or reject each other's suggestions, and can give clues if all else fails.
- Learners take a section of the mind map and explain the connections between the different entries. At a higher level, this could take the form of brief lectures for trainees in the learners' field.

Notes

One-to-one lessons

This activity is also suitable for individual lessons as it stands.

Learning techniques

Draw learners' attention to the usefulness of the mind map format for vocabulary revision and self-testing purposes.

Word families

Learners often know a noun without knowing the verb, adjective or adverb that goes with it, and vice versa. As a result, each of these closely-related words has to be learned separately.

This activity shows how words and their derivatives can be organized for easier memorizing and revision. It can also be used as a warm-up or follow up to text work.

Preparation

Level

Intermediate to advanced

Language

- The *organize* word family: *organize; organizer; organized; disorganized; unorganized; organization; organizational, etc.*
- Other word families that would be useful to your learners, e.g. *produce; sell; manage; succeed; economize; decide*

Before the lesson

1. Prepare a few sentences, each including at least one of the *organize* word family and preferably related to your learners' work.
2. Draw up three or four other word families that would be useful to your learners (see **Language**) and note the stress patterns on individual words.

You will need

- one copy of Worksheet A2.1 per learner;
- copies of Worksheet A2.2 for follow-up work;
- dictionaries.

The Activity

Introduction

1. Write the word *organize* on the board. Elicit *organizer*, e.g. by asking "What's the word for someone who organizes?" and write it below *organize*.
2. Ask if anyone knows any other words that start the same way and list them on the board too.
3. Check that learners know how the words in the list should be stressed, as this can vary considerably in a word family. You could do this by asking learners to group words according to their stress pattern, e.g.

Ooo	*organize, organized*
Oooo	*organizer*
oooOo	*organization*
oooOoo	*organizational*
oOoo	*disorganized, unorganized*
ooooOo	*disorganization*

4. Check that everyone in the class knows how to use the different words in the family. This could be done by supplying definitions, making true / false statements or giving gapped sentences, for example: "This word means a person who has to make things work efficiently;" "This company is a very small organization;" "We discuss (*organisational*) problems at our weekly meetings."

Note that:
- a word family can contain more than one noun, adjective, opposite, etc;
- stress can change according to context;
- a word can have different uses, for instance *organization* can mean the process or the structure;
- families can sometimes be extended by adding a prefix, as with *reorganize.*

Development

1. Select two or three new words (see **Language**) and write them on the board.
2. Divide the class into pairs. Give each pair one of the words and ask them to draw up a word family for it, using a dictionary if necessary.
3. When they have finished, pairs write their families on the board and answer any questions from other learners.
4. Hand out one copy of Worksheet A2.1 to each learner and ask them to record the word families that have come up so far. They can do this either in grammatical categories (see *organize* on the worksheet), by embedding words in personalized sentences or however else they find them easiest to remember and find. The four cards on the worksheet can be cut out and filed, though learners will probably find it easier to use proper filing cards. There are four more cards on Worksheet A2.2 if you need them.

Production

Working in small groups, learners produce a gapped text or set of statements for another group to complete. The words gapped should be taken from several different families on the board.

Further ideas

- Warm-up for work on a text:
  Select members of various word families from the text and write them on the board. Learners organize them into families (and perhaps add to them) and then predict the contents of the text. Go on to exploit the text in whatever way you have planned (see **Section B: Company Materials** for some ideas).
- Follow-up to work on a text:
  Learners identify and add to members of word families found in the text (they might need one word from each family as starters). They could then use the words to give an oral summary of (part of) the text.

Notes

One-to-one lessons

This activity can also be used in individual lessons. The dictionary work should still be done independently by the learner despite the fact that this will result in periods of silence; it is after all productive silence.

Learning techniques

Draw learners' attention to the usefulness of the word family format for vocabulary building, storage and reference purposes. Learners who come into contact with English outside lessons can be given copies of Worksheet A2.2 and encouraged to build up their own bank of word families, checking them with you from time to time.

Word partnerships

Many learners have sizeable vocabularies but are unable to form the combinations of words that are so essential to effective communication.
This activity shows business learners how they can get more out of the words they know and is also a good way of introducing new vocabulary.

Preparation

Level

Elementary to advanced

Language

Word partnerships:
- Noun-noun: e.g. *company headquarters*
- Adjective-noun: e.g. *a middle-sized company*
- Verb-noun: e.g. *to manage a company*
- Combinations of the above: e.g. *to manage a leading company*

Before the lesson

Choose one or two other words that your learners are familiar with (for instance *market; sales; product*) and draw up word partnerships for them.

You will need

- one copy of Worksheet A3.1 per learner;
- copies of Worksheet A3.2 for follow-up work;
- board markers in various colours.

The Activity

Introduction

1. Write the word *company* on the board. Surround it with three words which can precede it (e.g. *manage / middle-sized / parent*) in one colour and three which can follow it (e.g. *headquarters / results / policy*) in another.
2. Learners work out why the words are in different colours. Check that they have all got the right idea by asking them to produce sentences including the new word partnerships.

Development

1. Now write the components of a number of other *company* partnerships on the board, but without colour clues.
2. Working in pairs, learners create as many further partnerships (of two or more words) as they can, for instance:
   - *company news / regulations / logo;*
   - *a leading / profitable / multinational company;*
   - *to join / invest in / take over a company;*
   - *to plan company policy; to work for a well-known manufacturing company.*
3. Pairs report back to the rest of the class. Collect their partnerships on the board and draw attention to any that have not yet come up.

4. Learners record the partnerships they want to remember on their copies of Worksheet A3.1 They can use the box at the top of the worksheet to make a quick note of the new combinations but should also record them in full personalized sentences below and check these with you in due course. There is a blank version of the worksheet on A3.2.

Production

Learners prepare and make brief presentations on some aspect of their company's history or activities, or those of a competitor, using as many of the new partnerships as possible. This could be done as a business news programme, with each learner contributing a report or comment on the current business scene (see also **D4: Taking part in meetings**). With low-level groups this could be simplified to a set of statements.

Further idea

Find a text that includes vocabulary relevant to your learners' work, such as an excerpt from a company brochure or manual, a letter or an advertisement. Learners identify word partnerships and record them. Each learner then summarizes part of the text in his or her own words, incorporating the new partnerships.

Notes

One-to-one lessons

This activity can also be used in individual lessons, with the learner doing the brainstorming and preparation work alone.

Learning techniques

Draw learners' attention to the usefulness of this approach to vocabulary building. Encourage learners who come into contact with English outside lessons to build up their own bank of partnerships and check them with you from time to time.

"We're a parent company, Wolper – not to be confused with your real parents."

Starter phrases

Many otherwise competent communicators perform less effectively than they might because they make insufficient use of 'softening' expressions when requesting something or giving unwelcome information.

Although the phrases in this activity would not normally be thought of as vocabulary items, they can easily be learned as 'chunks', without worrying about their grammatical structure or functional category. This activity shows how a handful of such phrases can be used in a variety of different situations.

Preparation

Level

Elementary to advanced

Language

- 'Starter phrases', e.g. *I'd like to …; Would you mind …; I'm afraid …; Could I …?*
- Structures following starters, e.g. *I'd like to (make an appointment with …)*
- Possible responses, e.g. *Certainly*

Before the lesson

Choose a few starters that are relevant to your learners' field of activity and make a list of different ways in which they can be made into complete sentences. You will need at least one full sentence for every two learners in your class.

You will need

- one copy of Worksheet A4.1 per learner;
- copies of Worksheet A4.2 for follow-up work.

The Activity

Introduction

Write *I'd like to …* on the board. Elicit ways of completing the sentence and add them to the starter, for instance:

I'd like to	*make an appointment with Mrs Waters.* *introduce John Rowlands.* *show you around the factory.* *confirm my reservation for flight number …* *start by welcoming …*

Development

1. Discuss and practise the intonation and stressing of the sentences.
2. Hand out one copy of Worksheet A4.1 to each learner and ask them to write in the completed sentences.
3. Discuss situations in which the completed sentences could be used and elicit appropriate responses. This could be an opportunity to exploit another phrase, such as *I'm afraid …* or *Could I …?*

Production

Divide the class into pairs. Ask each pair to choose one of the sentences and responses and develop them into a dialogue. Pairs then play out their dialogues for the rest of the class.

Further ideas

- Learners match several different starters with a mixed bag of endings.
- Higher-level learners consider how a change of intonation can affect the message. They then devise role plays to contrast the effects of acceptable and unaccceptable intonation.

Notes

One-to-one lessons

This activity can also be used in individual lessons, but you will need to take part in the roleplay. You will be freer to concentrate on the task if you record this. You can then use the recording for correction work later.

Learning techniques

Draw learners' attention to the starter phrase format for phrase-building, storage and reference purposes. Encourage learners who come into contact with English outside lessons to build up their own bank of starters and check them with you from time to time.

Testing vocabulary

Many adult learners, especially those with stressful jobs, find that their retention of new language improves considerably if it is tested at regular intervals.

This activity demonstrates a test format that is flexible, fun and low on preparation time.

Preparation

Level

Beginners to advanced

Language

Any vocabulary you want to test

Before you start

Make yourself a copy of one of the tables on Worksheet A5. In the boxes, write 20 words or expressions you want to test.

You will need

one copy of Worksheet A5 for the whole class.

The Activity

Introduction

1. Copy the table on Worksheet A5 onto the board, but without the words you are going to test.
2. Divide the class into two teams. The learners in each team take it in turns to answer the questions.Toss a coin to decide which team will start.
3. A member of the first team names a square (e.g. *B3*). Look at your table and describe the word or expression you have written in that square. You could do this by saying, for instance:
   - *This is a word that means …*
   - *This is the opposite of / a synonym for …*
   - *This is the noun / verb / adjective of …*
   - *This word is missing from the following sentence: …*

   If the person who chose the square answers the question correctly, the team gets two points. If not, the question passes to rest of the team who have a chance to come up with a joint answer for one point.
4. Someone in the second team now chooses a square, and so on until all the squares have been dealt with. The team with the most points wins.

Development

1. Cut a copy of Worksheet A5 in half and give each team one of the tables.
2. Ask the teams to think of 20 words they have had in recent lessons and write them in their tables (for lower-level learners, two or three lines of the table will probably be enough, i.e. 8-12 words). Each member of the team should be prepared to describe at least one of the words in the table.

Production

Each team now tests the other on the words it has prepared.

Further idea

This activity also lends itself well to testing a wider range of language. Instead of A, B, C, D, head the columns in the table: Vocabulary, Grammar, Phrases, Surprise. Test vocabulary as above.

Grammar can be tested simply by saying: "Make a sentence including *isn't going to* (or *efficiently / have produced / often,* etc)." This will tell you a) whether the meaning is clear and b) whether learners know how to use the form in context.

To test Phrases (= functional language), ask: "Someone says *How are you?* (or *Thank you very much. / Could I use your phone?,* etc). What would you answer?"

The Surprise column can be used to test spelling, pronunciation, numbers, date and time, intercultural pitfalls and anything else you think necessary.

Notes

Using this activity at different levels

It might be easier to let very low-level learners answer all the questions as a team.

One-to-one lessons

This activity is not suitable for individual lessons.

Section B
Business Materials

1. Brochures
2. Manuals
3. Correspondence
4. Advertisements
5. Newspapers

Business organizations generate and make use of a wide range of written matter. Used as course material, this can help the teacher to focus closely on the learner's company and its activities and so make lessons more appropriate and relevant.

The main aim of the activities in this section is to give learners the confidence to read such authentic materials for the general sense, without worrying unduly about unfamiliar words and structures.

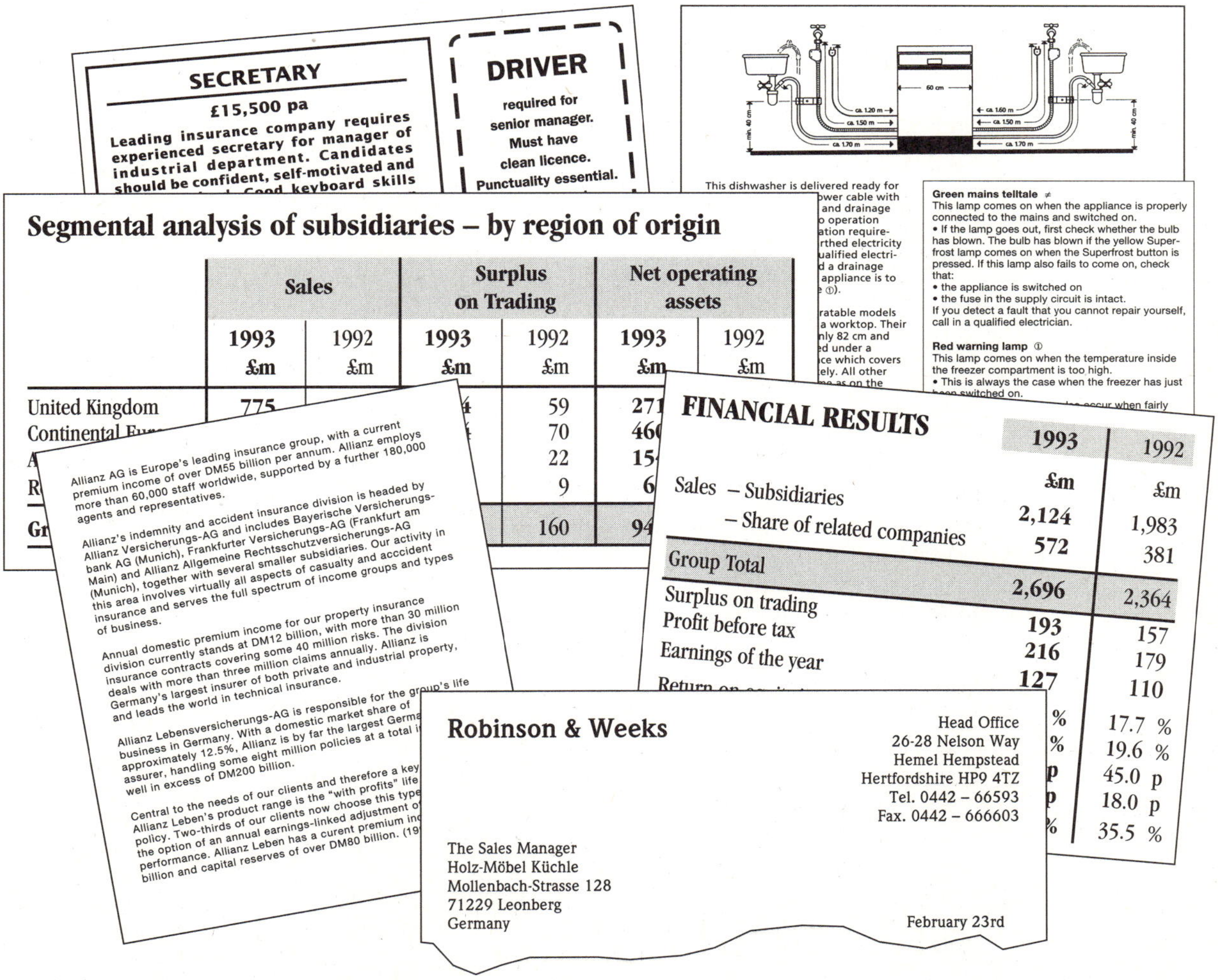

Brochures

Brochures are designed to promote a company and / or its products. Many international companies now produce their brochures in English as well as in their own language. These are an excellent source of appropriate text.

In this activity, learners read brochure texts for general meaning and specific information. They go on to find ways of making their texts easier to understand.

Preparation

Level

Elementary to advanced

Language

- Giving opinions: *We think ...; In our view, ...; We felt that ...*
- Giving reasons: *because (of); so*
- Word partnerships and other key items in the text you decide to use (see **A3: Word partnerships**)

Before the lesson

1. Find out whether your learners' company produces English versions of its brochures and ask them to get you copies (see the **Notes** section at the end of this activity for ways of using brochures in other languages).
2. Select a piece of text from a brochure. Ideally, it should be written in several short paragraphs and without headings (see Worksheet B1 for an example).

You will need

- one copy of the text you have decided to use per learner;
- two rooms or enough space between the teams so that they can discuss the same text without distracting each other.

The Activity

Introduction

1. Warm up by brainstorming the sort of information that is usually found in brochures.
2. Divide the class into two teams. Hand out one copy of the text to each learner.
3. Ask learners to read their texts quickly for the general sense. Set a time limit and do not answer questions about vocabulary yet.

Development

1. Working in their teams, learners discuss a suitable title for the text and headings for each paragraph. These should be brief and memorable rather than comprehensive. During this phase you could answer two or three vocabulary questions per team.
2. Still in their teams, learners look at the text again and devise one or more illustrations for each paragraph. These could be photographs, drawings, diagrams, maps or whatever else the team thinks appropriate.

Production

Each team now presents its suggestions for titles / headings and illustrations in turn. The audience should ask for details, explanations and justifications.

Further ideas

- Learners look at their texts again and identify useful word partnerships (see **A3: Word partnerships**).
- Ask learners to turn over their texts. Hand out a copy of the same text (or show it on an overhead projector) with important words / expressions blanked out. Working in pairs, learners complete the text from memory.
- Learners reconstruct the text from a few key phrases.

Notes

Using this activity at different levels

This activity is most effective at intermediate level and above. It can also be used succcessfully with lower-level learners as long as the text is relatively compact and it is quite clear that they are not expected to understand every word. In fact, it can be very motivating for such learners to find that they can get useful information from totally authentic material. More advanced classes could be challenged by being given the text on cassette only at first and asked to identify the source from the type of language used.

One-to-one lessons

This activity can also be used in individual lessons as it stands, except that the presentation will be made to you. Less-confident learners can record this while you are out of the room. You can then evaluate the finished product together.

Follow-up

This activity can be repeated at intervals with different extracts and focusing on different language features on each occasion.

Brochures in other languages

A lot of useful work can also be done with brochures that are not available in English. Photographs, drawings and diagrams can be described, explained and discussed, texts can be summarized in straightforward English, technical data and statistics used for work on numbers, and addresses of agencies, branches and subsidiaries for spelling practice.

Manuals

Although the language of manuals can look daunting, it typically consists of very restricted and predictable grammar and a limited set of recurring vocabulary. In this activity, learners identify some of the 'building blocks' of manuals language and use them to describe procedures in their own company.

Preparation

Level

Elementary to advanced

Language

Some examples commonly found in manuals:

- Descriptions: *The appliance is delivered with hoses and cable attached.*
- Imperatives: *Type in your code word; Do not remove the cover.*
- Possibilities: *This card can be used in any standard dispenser.*
- Obligations: *The safety bar must be lowered before operation.*
- Prohibitions: *Electrical components should not come into contact with water.*
- Conditional clauses: *The boiler shuts down automatically if the temperature limit is exceeded.*
- Time clauses: *This lamp comes on when the appliance is properly connected.*
- *'ing'* form after prepositions: *Open the file by clicking on the relevant symbol.*
- Other conventional expressions: *ready for (installation); (data) regarding (electrical connection); the relevant (setting); complies with (regulations).*

Before the lesson

Ask learners for a copy of the English manual(s) they are working with. Select a piece of text and identify recurring grammar features (see Worksheet B2 and **Language** above for examples). Decide which of these you want your learners to focus on and mark the sentences in which they occur.

You will need

one copy of the text you have decided to use per learner.

The Activity

Introduction

1. Warm up by brainstorming two or three characteristics of manuals (such as plain-looking, cheaply produced, clear line drawings, sometimes difficult to understand).
2. Ask learners to imagine a manual for a familiar piece of equipment (such as a car / PC / photocopier / walkman / freezer). Brainstorm a few typical sentences and write them on the board, rephrasing them in 'manuals style' as necessary, for example:
   - *Check that the handbrake is on and that the gears are in neutral.*
   - *Meat should not be put back in the freezer once it has been defrosted.*
   - *If the programme symbol does not come up on the screen, call the operator.*

   Note that these sentences already contain much of the typical grammar of manuals.

Development

1. Clean the board and write up headings for the types of sentence you want learners to find (e.g. Possibilities, Obligations, Prohibitions).
2. Hand out one copy of the text to each learner. Elicit one or two sentences to check that they are on the right track.
3. Working alone, learners read the text and underline all the examples they can find before comparing with a partner.
4. Collect learners' findings on the board under the relevant headings. Draw attention to the structures you want them to use.

Production

1. Elicit a few processes that are familiar to all your learners. If, as sometimes happens, the class is made up of staff from very different departments, focus on procedures well-known throughout the company (such as overtime, holiday and sickness regulations).
2. Divide the class into small groups. Each group chooses a different process or procedure and writes a piece of manuals text for it, including as many examples as possible of the structures they have been looking at *plus* one or two factual errors.
3. Groups read their texts to one another and try to spot the deliberate mistakes.

Further ideas

- Learners dictate an excerpt from a manual to one another, leaving out key expressions which their partners have to identify and recall.
- Learners reformulate a flow chart (see **C3: Flow charts**) as a text from a manual or vice versa.
- Learners reformulate an excerpt from a manual as speech. Higher-level learners could do this as a presentation (see **D2: Structuring a presentation**).

Notes

Using this activity at different levels

With very low level learners, you may want to limit the **Introduction** phase of this activity to the first step and just discuss the sort of language involved. More advanced learners could be asked to scan texts for recurring features themselves.

One-to-one lessons

This activity can be used in individual lessons as it stands, except for the partner and group work. In the **Production** phase, the learner should write only accurate information.

Follow-up

This activity can be repeated at intervals with different extracts and focusing on different language features on each occasion.

Correspondence

Business correspondence is generally written in a predictable format and using a restricted range of formulaic expressions.

In this activity, learners read correspondence for the essential facts and assemble straightfoward letters themselves.

Preparation

Level

Elementary to advanced

Language

- Conventional salutations and complimentary closes: *Dear Sir or Madam; Dear Mr / Mrs / Ms; Yours faithfully / sincerely,*
- Formulaic structures used in business letters, e.g. *we were interested to see; we would be grateful if; at your earliest convenience; we look for-ward to*
- Standard abbreviations, e.g. *ref; pp; encl.*

Before the lesson

Ask your learners for samples of the correspondence that causes them problems. Details that should not be seen by someone from outside the company can be blanked out.

You will need

- one copy of Worksheet B3.1 per learner;
- one copy of Worksheet B3.2 per learner;
- overhead transparencies of Worksheet B3.1 and a completed version of Worksheet B3.2 would be helpful but are not essential.

The Activity

Introduction

1. Warm up by eliciting the elements of any of business letter.
2. Write the following on the board in random order:

The writer's company	*The signature*
The complimentary close	*The main message*
Further questions or information	*A sketch of the writer's company*
The addressee	*The date of the letter*
The writer's name	*The salutation*
The writer's job title or department	*The reason for the letter*

3. Hand out one copy of Worksheet B3.1 to each learner or show it on the overhead projector. Ask learners to read the letter in pairs and identify the different elements listed on the board.
4. Pairs report their results to the class and / or mark the relevant parts of the letter on the OHP transparency. Note that in this case someone has signed the letter on behalf of the writer.
5. Clean the board or switch off the OHP. Working together, the class rewrite the letter in straightforward English. Write their version on the board, helping with vocabulary only when absolutely essential.

Key (one possible version)

Our company has got a lot of shops which sell furniture and other things for the home in Britain.

We were in Germany a few (days) ago and saw some of the things you make and thought they looked good and were well made. Please send us some information about them as soon as possible and tell us how much they cost, how you send them to customers and how to pay for them.

Please tell us how much you can take off the price if we order a lot, too.

We hope you will write soon.

Development

1. Clean the board / switch off the OHP and ask learners to turn over their worksheets. Write the following on the board:

Dear	*together with*
We are	*Perhaps you could*
specializing in	*you would be able to*
recent visit to	*We look forward to*
we were interested to	*Yours*
we would be grateful if	

2. Working in pairs, learners reconstruct the letter from memory. Allow plenty of time for this. Give praise for comprehensible results and do not worry about minor details.

Production

1. Clean the board. Ask learners to discuss what the contents of a reply to the above letter would be.
2. Hand out one copy of Worksheet B3.2 to each learner and ask them to complete it as they think best.
3. Learners compare their versions of the second letter and identify the formulaic language it uses. Ensure they realize that this is more or less invariable and that they do not need to worry about its grammar.

Key (one possible version)

Dear Mr ***Foley****,*

Thank you for ***your letter/enquiry*** *of* ***February 23rd***

We are pleased to send you copies of ***our (current) catalogue*** *and* ***(current) price list****. We would be able to offer you a* ***discount*** *of* ***(?)****% on all orders with a value of DM* ***(?)*** *or more.*

Please also find enclosed full details of ***our delivery service*** *and* ***terms of payment****.*

If you require any further ***information/details****, please do not hesitate to contact us.*

We ***look forward to*** *receiving your order.*

Yours *sincerely,*

Draw attention to the change in salutation and complimentary close when the writer knows the addressee's name.

Further ideas

- Learners personalize the letters in this activity by writing enquiries and replies from their own company to a possible supplier.
- Learners reassemble a letter which has been broken down into individual sentences / parts of sentences and jumbled.
- Learners separate and reassemble two letters which have been broken down into paragraphs and jumbled.
- Each learner receives details to be incorporated into a letter, which is then passed to a partner for reply.
- Learners transform a telephone call into an exchange of letters.

Notes

Using this activity at different levels

Higher-level learners could be asked to brainstorm all the elements in the second step of the **Introduction** phase. They can be given shorter, fewer or no prompts at all with which to reconstruct the letter in the **Development** phase.

One-to-one lessons

This activity can be used in individual lessons as it stands, except that the learner will have to do the pair and group tasks alone.

Follow-up

Learners who have to write business letters in English themselves will find it helpful to repeat this activity from time to time, analyzing a different type and style of letter on each occasion. Although this particular activity only looks at one exchange of letters, the basic approach can be used with any piece of correspondence.

Advertisements

Advertisements often contain useful company-related vocabulary. They also usually try to convey an image of the company behind the advertisement.

In this activity, learners read staff recruitment advertisements for the general sense and identify typical recruitment language. They go on to practise this in interview roleplays.

Preparation

Level

Intermediate to advanced

Language

- Vocabulary of advertisements, e.g.

  Recruitment: *salary; applicant; position; qualifications; experience; CV*
  Company self-portraits: *leading; fast-growing; forward-looking; based in*
  Job descriptions: *challenging; imagination; responsible*
  Qualification and personal qualities: *skills; knowledge of; self-motivated; outstanding*
- Modals verbs and other structures expressing ability and necessity: *should be; must have; will be able to; would be an advantage; are essential*

Before the lesson

1. Decide whether you are going to use Worksheet B4.1 or advertisements of your own. Note: On the worksheet, *32k* = £32,000 (*k* for *kilo*).
2. Decide which vocabulary items you are going to pre-teach and which you want your learners to guess from the context.

You will need

- one copy per learner of Worksheet B4.1 or your own advertisement(s);
- one copy per learner of Worksheet B4.2.

The Activity

Introduction

Brainstorm the sort of information that is normally included in a recruitment advertisement. Elicit the categories on Worksheet B4.2 and write them on the board.

Development

1. Hand out one copy of Worksheet B4.1 (or your own advertisements) to each learner. Working in pairs, they read the advertisements quickly to see whether they actually include the various categories of information written on the board. Encourage them to concentrate on the overall sense at this stage and not worry about individual words they may not know.
2. Now ask the pairs to look at the advertisements again and find expressions to fit the categories. Start them off with one or two examples (see **Language**).
3. Collect the expressions they come up with on the board and check the pronunciation.

4. Hand out one copy of Worksheet B4.2 to each learner and ask them to write down the examples from the board.

Production

1. Learners now choose one of the advertisements and brainstorm the sort of questions and answers that might come from both sides in an interview for the post.
2. Divide the class into two groups. One group prepares to play the interviewers for the job and the other the interviewees.
3. Learners now play out the interviews. Set a time limit for each candidate, for instance ten minutes. Recording the interviews usually makes evaluation easier.

Further ideas

- Learners write a recruitment advertisement for their own job, or for another post in their own department or organization.
- Learners write letters applying for one of the jobs advertised, as themselves or someone else.
- Learners prepare two CVs for one of the jobs advertised, one appropriate and the other not.

Notes

One-to-one lessons

This activity can be used in individual lessons if you play one of the interview roles. You will be freer to do this if you record the interview and use it for correction work later. You may however prefer to replace the interview with one of the **Further ideas**.

Other types of advertisement

Similar work can be carried out with product advertisements produced by the learners' company or its competitors. In this case, learners would focus on the vocabulary of the product and its qualities, and go on to discuss the style and effectiveness of the advertisement itself. This could be followed up with a roleplay of a sale or a meeting to discuss follow-up advertisements and promotional activities.

Newspapers

Many business people keep up to date with newspapers devoted to business affairs such as 'The Financial Times' or 'The Wall Street Journal'. Other papers, such as 'The European', have substantial business sections.

This activity encourages learners to read English-language newspapers as they would one in their own language, *scanning* for areas of interest and *skimming* for the main points of a story.

Preparation

Level

Elementary to advanced

Before the lesson

1. Divide a newspaper so that there is at least one page for each pair of learners.
2. Write a quiz (see example below). Each page of the newspaper should contain the answer to at least one of the questions.

An example of a newspaper quiz

> 1. *What is the rate of the (currency) against the (currency)?*
> 2. *What is the (inflation/unemployment/interest rate) in (country)?*
> 3. *What was the price of (company)'s shares?*
> 4. *What was the trend in the (country) stock market?*
> 5. *What is the problem at (company)?*
> 6. *Why is (government/company/individual) ...ing?*
> 7. *How much is (government/company/individual) going to invest in (company)?*
> 8. *Why does (government/company/individual) think ...?*
> 9. *What does the journalist think about ...?*
> 10. *Find a headline that means ...*

You will need

- one copy of a business newspaper for the class (there should be at least one page for every pair of learners);
- one copy of the quiz (see **Before the lesson**) for every pair of learners.

The Activity

1. Divide the class into pairs and give each pair a copy of the quiz you have prepared (see **Before the lesson**).
2. Separate the pages of the newspaper and put them in the centre of the table or classroom.
3. Each pair of learners takes a page, works through it and replaces it in the centre. The first pair to find all ten pieces of information wins.

Further ideas

- Learners scan the paper for an interesting-looking article and read it. They then report the information it contains in their own words and answer questions from the class.

- Cut out five to six articles and separate their headlines. Learners read the articles through and match them with the appropriate headlines.
- Give each pair of learners a different photograph or diagram from the paper and ask them to devise a story to go with it.
- Learners look for two advertisements, one that seems to offer a credible product or service and one that does not. They then describe the advertisements and justify their impressions.

Notes

Using this activity at different levels

You may decide that it is enough for lower-level learners to find information and say which page it was on, or identify people / things in given photographs. Higher-level learners can be challenged by being asked to find more obscure information and comment on it.

One-to-one lessons

This activity is suitable for individual lessons as it stands. You might however want to set a time limit as there is no one to race against.

Section C
Business Diagrams

1. **Organigrams**
2. **Pie charts**
3. **Flow charts**
4. **Grids**
5. **Bar charts**

Much business information comes these days in visual form, and absorbing and processing facts presented in this way is second nature to most business people. However, there are situations where the information conveyed in a diagram has to be turned into speech - on the telephone, for instance - or clarified and commented on in some way, as in presentations.

This section looks at some of the most common types of business diagram, and shows how they can be used in the classroom. Integrating diagrams into business presentations is dealt with in **D2: Presenting visual information**. Graphs are also described in the same activity.

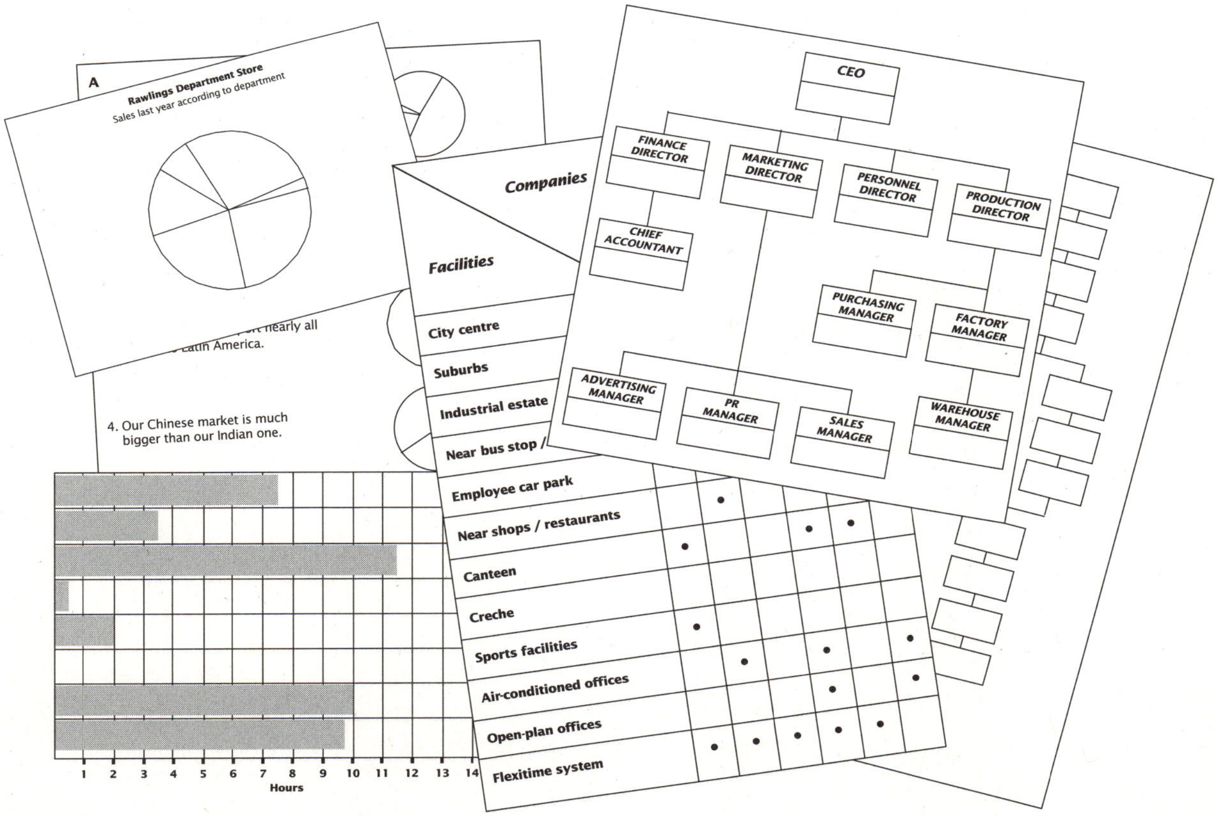

Organigrams

An organigram shows the basic structure of an organization, with its lines of communication and responsibility. In this activity, learners use organigrams to describe the structure of their own department or company.

Preparation

Level

Elementary to advanced

Language

- Job titles: *chief executive; marketing director; sales manager; boss; assistant*
- Names of divisions and departments: *personnel; sales; accounts department*
- Expressing responsibility: *to be the head of / in charge of / responsible for / responsible to; to report to*

Before the lesson

Ask for an organigram of your learners' organization. These can often be found in company brochures and annual reports.

You will need

- one copy of Worksheet C1.1 per learner;
- one copy of Worksheets C1.2 and C1.3 per pair of learners.

The Activity

Introduction

1. Warm up by brainstorming the management titles / department names common to most companies, for example CEO *(chief executive officer), director, manager, finance, marketing, personnel,* and collect them on the board.
2. Hand out one copy of Worksheet C1.1 to each learner. Ask them to read the text and write the relevant management titles or department names in the organigram.

Key

1st line: *CEO*
2nd line: *finance director, marketing director, personnel director, production director*
3rd line: *chief accountant*
4th line: *purchasing manager, factory manager*
5th line: *warehouse manager*
6th line: *advertising manager, PR manager, sales manager*

Development

1. Divide the class into pairs. Hand out a copy of Worksheet C1.2 to one of the learners in each pair and C1.3 to the other. Both learners now have the same organigram, and between them they also have twelve sentences which will help them to establish the personal names of the managers in the diagram.
2. Learners take it in turns to read out one of their six sentences to their partners and write the information they hear in their organigrams.

Key

1st line: *Mr Thomas*
2nd line: *Mr Forrest, Mrs Hill, Mr Baker, Mr Stone*
3rd line: *Mrs Richards*
4th line: *Mr Peterson, Mr Daniel*
5th line: *Mr Clark*
6th line: *Mr Browning, Ms Alexander, Mrs Wilkie*

Production

Each pair now presents an organigram of their own company to another pair. They can do this using either the official company organigram (for instance, from a brochure or annual report) or their own versions, as they prefer. Learners who work for the same company could describe fictional organizations. While one pair is presenting its diagram, the other draws what is being described. The two can then be compared.

Further ideas

- Learners write up the organigram as a text.
- Learners fill gaps in a written description of the organigram.
- Learners find the deliberate mistakes in a dictated description of the organigram.
- Learners who work for a company whose organization has changed significantly at some point (for instance through a merger or takeover) could draw the original structure on the board and explain the subsequent changes to newer employees, who alter the diagram accordingly.
- More advanced learners could compare their company organization with that on the worksheets, using expressions such as *both, neither, however, on the other hand,* etc.

Notes

One-to-one lessons

This activity can be used in individual lessons as it stands except that you will have to act as the partner in the information exchanges. You will be freer to concentrate on the task if you record these. You can then use the recording for correction work later.

Pie charts

Pie charts are used to show individual elements in relation to a whole, for example the number of employees in the different departments of a company as percentages of the total workforce, or the performance of various products as proportions of sales.

In this activity, learners use pie charts to make comparisons and describe proportion and relative significance.

Preparation

Level

Intermediate to advanced

Language

- Number: *cardinal numbers, percentages, fractions, price*
- Comparison: *more ... than; bigger ... than; most; biggest; smallest*
- Modification: *about (two-thirds); a little (more); much (bigger); nearly (all the rest)*

Before the lesson

Find out whether there are any pie charts in the promotional materials or reports produced by your learners' company.

You will need

- one copy of Worksheet C2.1 per learner;
- one copy of Worksheets C2.2 and C2.3 per pair of learners.

The Activity

Introduction

Hand out one copy of Worksheet C2.1 to each person in the class. Learners read the short texts in A and match them with the four pie charts on the right. They then read the longer text in B and complete the empty pie chart.

Key

1st text: *fourth chart*
2nd text: *first chart*
3rd text: *second chart*
4th text: *third chart*

Development

1. Brainstorm the sorts of things one can buy in a department store. Organize them into departments (food, furniture, fabrics, lighting, DIY, sports, stationery, etc) and list them on the board.
2. Divide the class into pairs and hand out one copy of Worksheet C2.2 to one of the learners in each pair and C2.3 to the other. Learners look at the first pie chart on their worksheets and decide which of the segments should represent the sales of which department, but without telling their partner.
3. Learners complete their empty pie charts by asking their partners for the missing information. When they have finished, they compare results.

Production

1. Each learner now draws a pie chart, preferably on a company-related topic, for example:
   – sales of different products in relation to total sales;
   – relative size of various markets;
   – number of employees in different departments.

   Charts with this sort of information can usually be found in company brochures and reports but learners can of course design their own if they prefer or these are not available.
2. Learners take it in turns to present the information contained in their chart to the rest of the class, but without showing them the diagram itself. As they listen, the other learners try to draw an appropriate chart.

Further ideas

- Learners take the information from a pie chart and write it up as a text.
- Learners take the information from a text and turn it into a pie chart.
- Learners compare two or more pie charts conveying the same sort of information from different years, for example sales present and past.

Notes

One-to-one lessons

This activity can be used in individual lessons as it stands except that you will have to act as the partner in the information exchanges. You will be freer to concentrate on the task if you record these. You can then use the recording for correction work later.

Flow charts

Flow charts are used to represent processes and procedures. These can range from straightforward instruction sequences, such as how to deal with an invoice, to the parallel developments and special options one might find in a complex planning or production process.

In this activity, learners give step-by-step descriptions of familiar working routines and contingency procedures.

Preparation

Level

Intermediate to advanced

Language

- Sequence: *first of all; then; after that; next; before; as soon as; finally*
- Obligation: *you have to / don't have to; should*
- Condition: *if (you want to); when (you've finished)*
- Present Simple Passive

Before the lesson

Find out whether there are any flow charts in the promotional materials or manuals produced by your learners' company.

You will need

one copy of Worksheet C3 per learner.

The Activity

Introduction

1. Divide the class into pairs. Ask learners to call out any procedures they are familiar with (such as dealing with an invoice, answering a customer call, attending a meeting, or a production process) and collect them on the board. You will need at least one procedure for each pair of learners.
2. Learners describe the first few steps of one of the procedures. Write one or two of these on the board in note form (for example *1. pick up the phone; 2. say who you are ...*).
3. Each pair now chooses one of the procedures on the board and notes down the different steps involved. They will need this information later in the activity.

Development

Hand out one copy of Worksheet C3 to each learner. The worksheet shows a process both as a flow chart and as a set of written steps, each marked with a letter. The steps, however, are out of sequence. Learners read them, establish the correct order and enter the appropriate letter in the chart.

Key (from top to bottom)

g - l - i - a
c-m / e-h-j
b-f-d-k

Production

1. Still in pairs, learners choose one of the procedures on the board (see **Introduction**) and draw up a flow chart for it.
2. Pairs take it in turns to present their chart to the rest of the class, using as much of the language on Worksheet C3 as possible (they may need the Present Simple Passive here, especially if they are describing a production process). The audience should check to see whether any step or option in the process has been forgotten.

Further ideas

- Learners read a text and present the information it contains as a flow chart or vice versa.
- Working independently, all the learners in the class design flow charts for the same process and then compare results.
- Learners look at a simplified flow chart and decide what contingencies have not been covered and how they should be represented on the chart.

Notes

One-to-one lessons

This activity can be used in individual lessons as it stands except that you will have to act as the partner in the information exchanges. You will be freer to concentrate on the task if you record these. You can then use the recording for correction work later.

Drawing by Stevenson; © 1977; The New Yorker Magazine, Inc.

Grids

Grids are used to present the characteristics of a number of items so that they can be compared at a glance.

In this activity, learners use grids as a basis for making, linking and contrasting statements on a range of items.

Preparation

Level

Elementary to advanced

Language

- Quantity: *none / one / both / neither / some / most / all (of them)*
- Contrast: *although; on the other hand; nevertheless*
- Company facilities and working conditions, e.g. *open-plan office; canteen*

Before the lesson

Find out whether there are any grids in the promotional materials or manuals produced by your learners's company.

You will need

- one copy of Worksheets C4.1 and C4.2 per learner;
- one copy of Worksheet C4.3 per pair of learners.

The Activity

Introduction

1. Warm up by brainstorming company locations and facilities, and the advantages and disadvantages of working in central and suburban areas. Collect any useful vocabulary that comes up on the board.
2. Hand out one copy of Worksheets C4.1 and C4.2 to each learner. Learners complete the text with the help of the grid.

Key

1. *most*
2. *some*
3. *both*
4. *on the other hand*
5. *all*
6. *nevertheless*
7. *although*
8. *one*
9. *neither*
10. *none*

Development

1. Divide the class into pairs. Each pair makes as many *untrue* sentences about the grid as possible, using the words in the box. Set a time limit.
2. Each pair reads out a sentence in turn. The other learners check first of all that it is indeed untrue and then correct it. The pair with the most untrue sentences wins.

Production

1. Hand out one copy of Worksheet C4.3 to each pair, who use the empty grid to organise information on one of the following (or any other subject of their choice):
   – working conditions in their own and other companies;
   – advantages and disadvantages of different jobs;
   – strengths and weaknesses of various products.
2. Each pair exchanges its grid with another pair, who check that they understand the information it shows. They then prepare to present this information to the rest of the class, but without showing the grid itself.
3. During a presentation, the other learners listen and take notes, asking for clarification if necessary. The pair who supplied the grid check that the information being given is correct.
4. A volunteer now tries to reconstruct the original grid on the board with help from the rest of the class.

Further ideas

- Learners read a text and convert the information into a grid.
- Learners transfer information from a grid to another format, such as a letter, a telephone conversation or a dialogue from a meeting.
- Learners use information contained in a grid as the basis for a problem-solving activity; for instance, considering which of a number of firms should be asked to supply their organisations with services such as office cleaning, catering, security or professional training.

Notes

One-to-one lessons

This activity can be used in individual lessons as it stands, except that you will have to act as the partner in the information exchanges. You will be freer to concentrate on the task if you record these. You can then use the recording for correction work later.

Bar charts

Bar charts are used to contrast a number of totals, such as sales per year, output per factory or goods per household.

In this activity, learners use bar charts to establish the amount of time they spend on different tasks at work and talk about them.

Preparation

Level

Elementary to advanced

Language

- Work activities: *telephoning; writing letters; checking figures; attending meetings*
- Time (duration / fractions of hours): *two hours per day / week; six and a quarter hours*
- Modification: *at least / about / nearly / over / more or less / under (an hour)*

Before the lesson

Find out whether there are any bar charts in the promotional materials and reports produced by your learners' company.

You will need

one copy of Worksheets C5.1 and C5.2 per learner.

The Activity

Introduction

1. Warm up by asking learners to call out all the things they do at work. Collect them on the board in broad categories (see key below).
2. Hand out one copy of Worksheet C5.1 to each person in the class. Learners read the text and identify which of the bars represents which activity.

Key (from top to bottom)

telephoning
visitors
meetings
planning
letters
reading (0)
trip
report

3. Focus on the time expressions in the text *(at least one and a half hours, nearly ten hours, etc)* by asking learners how many they can find. Collect them on the board and see if anyone in the class can add to the list.

Development

1. Hand out one copy of Worksheet C5.2 to each learner. Learners draw bar charts showing the amount of time they spent on different work activities in the previous week.
2. Divide the class into pairs. Learners exchange their worksheets and write one sentence about each bar in their partner's chart, including duration expressions from the list on the board.

Production

Pairs join up with another pair and take it in turns to read out the sentences they have written. The new partners draw bar charts representing what they hear. They can ask for the sentences to be repeated but are not allowed to show their charts to the other pair until they have finished.

Further ideas

- Groups report their results to someone who draws a class chart on the board. Draw a scale on the side of the board, showing *none / one / a few / some / a lot / most / nearly all / all of us*. Groups now compete to produce as many sentences about the class as possible, using the words on the scale.
- Learners discuss the implications of their working weeks as revealed by the charts. They will probably want expressions of frequency such as *normally, several times a week* and *from time to time* for this.
- Learners could also draw up similar charts on the use of leisure time, holiday types and activities, etc.

Notes

One-to-one lessons

This activity can be used successfully with individual students up to the end of the Development phase if you act as the partner. Each of you would then read out your sentences in turn while the other decides whether they are accurate.

Section D
Business Skills

Doing business involves various basic communication skills such as being able to put people at their ease, get a message across in person as well as on paper, and guide a problem-solving discussion to a satisfactory outcome.

Business people - in particular managers - generally acquire such skills early on in their careers and then take them more or less for granted. Doing the same things effectively in a foreign language, however, can be a very different matter, as learners sometimes discover to their cost.

This section gives practice in some of the skills that many business learners have difficulty with.

Small talk

Successful business contacts depend on more than an ability to talk about the business itself: there are also the 'bits in between' when at least some attempt at personal conversation has to be made. Many otherwise confident business people find this difficult to do in another language.

In this activity, learners identify appropriate subjects and practise talking about them.

Preparation

Level

Elementary to advanced

Language

- Questions: e.g. *Where are you based?; How many people do you employ?*
- Tag questions: e.g. *You're part of the BLG Group, aren't you?*
- Responses: e.g. *Uh huh; Really?; That's interesting; I didn't know that.*

Before the lesson

Find out whether your learners have foreign visitors and where they travel themselves on business.

You will need

one copy of Worksheet D1 for each learner.

The Activity

Introduction

Brainstorm the following things and write them on the board:

- business situations when learners have to make small talk (such as collecting a visitor from reception and taking them to their office, waiting for a colleague to arrive and during breaks in meetings);
- things people know most about (such as their own company, job, region, town, home, family and personal interests);
- things a visitor can ask about (such as places to visit in the area, regional specialities, the local economy).

Development

1. Hand out one copy of Worksheet D1 to each learner. Ask them to fill in the left-hand column.
2. Working in pairs, learners now think of questions to get people talking about the topics they have written down.
3. Collect the questions on the board. Some possibilities would be:
   - *You're part of the BLG Group, aren't you?; How many people does your company employ?*
   - *How long have you been with the company?; Where are you based?*
   - *Newcastle's in northern England, isn't it?; What's it like?*
   - *Do you live in the city itself?; Have you got any children?*
   - *What do you do in your spare time?; How do you keep fit?*
4. Still in pairs, learners practise asking and answering questions. These can then be recorded in the right-hand column of the worksheet.

Production

1. Elicit the sort of 'interested response' that tells a speaker you are listening and keeps a conversation flowing (see **Language**). Write some examples on the board.
2. Learners form groups of three or four. Each group chooses a different small talk situation.
3. Group now roleplays their situations for the rest of the class. The winner is the group that can keep the conversation going longest or is votest best by the class.

Further ideas

- The restaurant
  Learners roleplay hosts and guests over a business lunch. Ask a confident learner to play the waiter / waitress, or do so yourself.
- The bar
  Learners roleplay business people relaxing at a hotel bar. Ask a confident learner to play the barkeeper, or do so yourself.
- The lift
  Create a lift by closing off a square area in the corner of the classroom with chairs or tables. Two learners enter the lift and keep up a conversation until the bell (played by you) pings, the doors open and more people get in. The new arrivals are now responsible for making conversation with everyone in the lift until it arrives at another floor, and so on. You decide who should enter or leave the lift and when.

Notes

Using this activity at different levels

Lower-level learners might find the roleplay easier if they write down a few prompt words on a card before starting, for instance *company size / location / job description / years with company / home town / family / hobbies.*

One-to-one lessons

This activity can also be used in individual lessons as it is, except that you will need to help lower-level learners with the questions in the **Development** phase and play the visitor in the roleplay.

"Mr Hoxbridge was just telling me that the first machine tool show for United States manufactures only was held in Cleveland, Ohio, in 1927."

Structuring a presentation

Business presentations are made for a variety of purposes: to describe an organization, to sell a product or to explain a policy or procedure. The aim is simply to transfer information to the audience as clearly and memorably as possible.

In this activity, learners consider the elements of a good presentation and collect appropriate language before going on to make presentations of their own. Talking about diagrams in presentations is dealt with in **D3: Presenting visual information**.

Preparation

Level

Elementary to advanced

Language

- Greeting / Identifying oneself: *Good morning. My name's ...; I'm from ...*
- Introducing the subject: *I'm here to talk about ...; I'd like to speak about ...*
- Describing the sequence: *First of all; secondly; then; next; after that; finally*
- Starting the presentation itself: *I'd like to start by ...; Right. Let's start with ...*
- Moving on to the next point: *Now let's turn to ...; Next, I'd like to look at ...*
- Summarizing: *In other words, ...; To put it in a nutshell, ...;To sum up, ...*
- Concluding: *Finally, ...; Let me conclude by ...*
- Thanking/Inviting questions: *Thank you. If you've got any questions ...*

Before the lesson

1. Find out what sort of presentations your learners have to give.
2. Have a list of topics available in case they cannot come up with one of their own, for example:
   - learner's company organization / history / prospects
   - a competitor's products / image / weaknesses
   - learner's job description / career to date / recent activities
   - (inter)national economic / industrial / social trends
   - learner's home town / area / region.

You will need

one copy of Worksheet D2 per learner.

The Activity

Introduction

1. Brainstorm the main steps in a typical presentation, for instance:
   a) Greet the audience.
   b) Say who you are and where you work.
   c) Say what you are going to talk about.
   d) Explain the order in which you will deal with different aspects of the topic.
   e) Start the presentation itself.
   f) Summarize each important point before going on to the next one.
   g) Summarize the whole message.
   h) Give your conclusions.
   i) Thank the audience for their attention.
   j) Invite questions.

2. Hand out one copy of Worksheet D2 to each learner. Working in small groups, learners brainstorm expressions for each step on the worksheet. Set a time limit.
3. Groups compare their results. Collect their ideas on the board, guiding and correcting as necessary (see Language for some suggestions).

Development

1. Ask each learner to choose a topic for a five-minute 'mini-presentation'. Allow about 15 minutes' preparation time. Go around the class, helping as necessary.
2. Learners give their presentations in turn, incorporating the expressions on their worksheets. The rest of the class listen and make notes on the language used.
3. Give feedback, concentrating on errors which would detract from the effectiveness of the message. Make sure learners realize that while accuracy is important, fluency is essential if they are to keep the audience's attention.

Production

1. Learners now prepare a full presentation. This could either be an expanded version of the one they have just given or a presentation on any other subject of their choice.
2. Each learner gives his or her presentation while the other members of the group take notes and prepare to ask one awkward question each at the end. Dealing with unexpected questions is probably the most worrying part of any presentation and learners should be given as much practice in this as possible.

Notes

Other forms of presentation

The sequence suggested in the **Introduction** phase is one that is widely used for formal and semi-formal presentations. There are of course other ways in which such information can be presented.

Timing

Depending on the size and level of the class, you will probably find that the **Introduction** and **Development** phases described above are enough for one lesson. Learners can be asked to prepare their full presentations for homework and make them in subsequent lesons.

Self-assessment

Ideally, presentations should be videoed so that learners can watch and assess their own performance. If this is not possible, an audio recording can also be very helpful.

Using this activity at different levels

Making a presentation is a useful activity at all levels from elementary onwards. It is a particularly good confidence-building exercise for lower-level learners, as it shows them that they can speak for extended periods rather than simply responding to questions or constructing single sentences. However, limit the language input at lower levels and do not expect the presentations to be very sophisticated. Weak or nervous learners could make team presentations, each member being responsible for one section of the topic.

Check what learners are doing in the preparation stages and see that they are not being over-ambitious. Make sure you give higher-level learners the feedback on stress and intonation they need to create the right personal impression and get their message across in the way they want.

One-to-one lessons

Record individual learners' presentations on video or audio cassette, so that they can self-correct and make their own assessment of their overall performance. You will of course be able to give more active help with preparation than in a group lesson, but be careful not to interfere too much. It is your learner's presentation and he or she should have the chance to prepare it independently. It does not matter if you are passive at this stage, giving help only when the learner asks for it.

Presenting visual information

Visual aids of various kinds - especially diagrams - are frequently used to illustrate points in business presentations and meetings.

This activity is designed to follow work on overall presentation structure done in the previous activity (**D2: Stucturing a presentation**). Here, learners describe the development of a graph and acquire language for integrating visual information of this kind into a presentation. Other types of diagram are dealt with in **Section C: Business diagrams**.

Preparation

Level

Intermediate to advanced

Language

- Describing graphs: *The horizontal / vertical axis shows ...*
- Describing trends: *stand at; rise / fall; slightly / gradually / sharply; reach a peak / the lowest point; level off; dip; fluctuate*
- Introducing a visual aid: *Let's have a look at ...; To illustrate this, I'd like to show you ...*
- Outlining the content: *Here we can see ...; This shows ...*
- Focussing: *I'd like to draw your attention to ...; The key factor is ...; Note ...*
- Emphasizing: *I'd like to emphasize ...; We shouldn't underestimate ...*
- Comparing: *On the other hand, ...; By comparison, ...; If we compare this with ..., we find ...*
- Drawing conclusions: *What does this tell us? Well, ...; In other words, ...; This means that ...*

Before the lesson

1. Decide whether you are going to use Worksheet D3.1 or graphs of your own. If you use your own graphs, you will need to write an accompanying text on the lines of the one on the worksheet.
2. Decide whether you want learners to use the functional categories on Worksheet D3.2 (see **Language** for suggested exponents) or others. The task in the **Development** phase will be more challenging if you include a few more exponents than you have categories.
3. Writing the exponents you want to present in the **Development** phase on an OHP transparency or flipchart sheet (concealed at first) will save time later.

You will need

- one copy per learner of Worksheet D3.1 (or your own graphs) per learner;
- one copy of Worksheet D3.2 per learner;
- an overhead projector with some blank transparencies would be useful when learners come to make their presentations, but they could also use the board or a flipchart.

The Activity

Introduction

1. Warm up by brainstorming the sort of visual aids that are most often used in presentations (see **Section C: Business diagrams**). If learners come up with a type of diagram that you are not familiar with, ask them to draw an example on the board and explain what it is used for.
2. Hand out one copy of Worksheet D3.1 (or your own graphs) to each learner. Working in pairs, learners read the text and underline all the expressions that describe movement and position (see **Language**). They then decide which of the three graphs the text refers to.
3. Still in pairs, learners take it in turns to describe the other two graphs to one another, using expressions from the text as necessary. Alternatively, learners could draw graphs of their own and 'dictate' them to their partners, who then draw what they hear. In this case, neither of the partners should see each other's drawings until they have completed the task.

Development

1. Ask learners to imagine they are listening to a manager reporting on his or her department's performance. Elicit exponents that he or she could use to introduce one of the graphs on Worksheet D3.1 (see **Language**).
2. Write the other exponents you want to teach on the board in random order. Working in pairs, learners discuss the function of each exponent but do not write anything yet.
3. Hand out one copy of Worksheet D3.2 to each learner. Still in pairs, learners match the exponents on the board with the categories on the worksheet. Check their results before they write them in. They can use the blank box to add any expressions they wish.
4. Ask each learner to draw one or two visuals aids (or find some they would like to describe in their company's publications).
5. Learners present their visuals to their partners, using the new language.

Production

1. Each learner now prepares a presentation including visuals language and incorporating structuring exponents from **D2: Presenting visual information**. These presentations could either be either expanded versions of what they did in the **Development** phase or be based on new topics. You will probably want to set this task for homework so that learners have enough time to prepare thoroughly. Organize the presentations over several lessons if necessary, rather than rushing them.
2. Learners make their presentations to the rest of the class. Each member of the audience should ask at least one question at the end.

Further ideas

- Each learner draws and presents a graph of a familiar product that typically has seasonal sales - such as skis, garden furniture or summer clothing - but without saying what it is. The class have to guess, giving their reasons. The presenter can only answer "*Yes*" or "*No*". This task could of course also be done with graphs from their own company's publications.
- Lower-level learners could be asked to present one of the diagrams in **Section C: Business Diagrams**.
- More advanced learners prepare and make presentations including several different types of diagram.

Notes

Self-assessment

As with the previous activity, these presentations should ideally be videoed so that learners can watch and assess their own performance. If this is not possible, an audio recording can also be very helpful.

Using this activity at different levels

Lower-level learners will probably not be familiar with all the language on Worksheet D3.1 but let them try to identify the relevant graph themselves before giving help. They may find the **Development** phase of the activity easier if they have first described *both* the graphs on the worksheet *and* their own versions (as in the alternative suggestion).

Higher-level learners could be challenged by having to present a visual aid supplied by their partner in the **Production** phase. They should also contribute alternative and further exponents of the language supplied.

One-to-one lessons

This activity can also be used with individual learners if you act as the partner in the third step of the **Introduction** phase.

Taking part in meetings

Business meetings can range from straightforward problem-solving sessions between close colleagues to formal gatherings with set procedures.

In this activity, learners acquire and practise a range of expressions which would be appropriate in most types of international meeting. The language required for guiding and controlling meetings is dealt with in **D5: Chairing a meeting**.

Preparation

Level

Intermediate to advanced

Language

- Giving opinions: *I'd say ...; As I see it, ...; In my experience, ...*
- Gaining time: *I'd just like to make two points: firstly, ...; There are several issues here: one, ...*
- Agreeing: *Yes, that's right; Exactly!*
- Disagreeing: *I'm not sure about that; With respect, ...; Yes, but ...*
- Reacting non-committally: *It depends. On the one hand ... on the other hand ...*
- Asking for clarification: *Sorry, could you repeat that?; I'm afraid I didn't quite understand; Could you give us an example?*
- Interrupting: *Can I come in here?*
- Dealing with interruptions: *Sorry, could I just finish?*

Before the lesson

Decide whether you want to ask your learners to suggest a topic for a meeting or use the idea described in the **Production** phase.

You will need

- one copy of Worksheet D4.1 (cut into 16 cards) per group of three to four learners;
- one copy of Worksheet D4.2 per learner.

The Activity

Introduction

1. Warm up by asking learners what sort of meetings they go to, how often and what their own role is.
2. Divide learners into groups of three or four. Write a typical 'discussions phrase' (such as *In my opinion)* on the board and ask the groups to think of some other expressions which *participants* often use during meetings. Avoid discussion of the chairperson's role here, as this is dealt with fully in the next activity.

Development

1. Hand out one set of cards from Worksheet D4.1 to each group. Ask them to organize the cards into eight categories (see **Language**).
2. Hand out one copy of Worksheet D4.2 to each learner. Still in groups, learners compare their categories with those on the worksheet. Check their decisions before they write the exponents on the worksheet.

Production

1. Collect all the cards, shuffle them and deal them out so that each learner has several.
2. Brainstorm:
   - three or four business stories in the news;
   - the names of a number of newspapers / magazines familiar to your learners.
3. Set up a TV business programme simulation. Learners play the journalist or business expert of their choice while you chair the discussion.
4. Introduce the programme as if you were on the air ("Good evening and welcome to 'Business Report'. With me today are ..."). Invite the participants to give their views on the various stories. Encourage discussion and dissent. Learners have to 'use up' their cards by incorporating the phrases on them in their contributions to the discussion. As each phrase is used, the speaker turns over the relevant card. Wind up the programme when all the cards have been used.

Further ideas

- Learners discuss and draw up a list of tips for participants in meetings.
- Learners brainstorm problems that can occur in international meetings, such as intercultural misunderstandings, and discuss solutions.

Notes

Self-assessment

Meetings should ideally be videoed so that learners can watch and assess their own performance. If this is not possible, an audio recording can also be very helpful.

Using this activity at different levels

If the categorizing task in the **Introduction** phase is too difficult for your learners, hand out Worksheet D4.2 at the same time as the cards or write the categories on the board.

Higher-level learners should be encouraged to contribute further expressions. One of them could also be asked to chair the final discussion, taking a known TV interviewer as a model.

One-to-one lessons

This activity can also be used with individual learners if they carry out the tasks on their own and the TV programme is changed into an interview (an imaginative learner could be asked to play several different interviewees). Most learners will also benefit from the opportunity to discuss the **Further ideas** above.

Follow-up

The **Production** phase of this activity can be reused at intervals, as learners acquire new language.

Chairing meetings

Chairing a meeting is as much a matter of giving it a perceptible structure as of guiding the discussion itself. A competent chairperson will prepare the meeting beforehand and follow up any decisions that are made. He or she will also take account of the mood and reactions of the participants as the meeting proceeds.

Not all learners have to chair meetings themselves but many need to be able to recognize and react to verbal signals used by the chairperson when they are participants.

This activity is designed to follow work on general meetings language done in the previous activity (**D4: Taking part in meetings**). Learners now consider some aspects of meetings-management and go on to identify and work with expressions used from the chair.

Preparation

Level

Intermediate to advanced

Language

- Opening the meeting: *Right. Shall we make a start?; I think we're all here, so ...*
- Outlining the aims of the meeting: *We're here to discuss ...; We've got three items on the agenda. Firstly, ...*
- Asking for opinions: *How do you see this?; What's your view?*
- Redirecting the discussion: *I think we should concentrate on ...; Perhaps we could get back to ...*
- Moving on to another point: *Let's look at the next point now; Can we move on to the second item on the agenda?*
- Asking for agreement: *Can we agree on this?; Are we all in favour?*
- Summarizing: *Right. Let me try to sum up; Let's see where we are.*
- Closing the meeting: *Well, I think that's as far as we can go at the moment. Thank you; Right, I think we've covered everything now, so ...*

Before the lesson

1. Make a list of suitable topics for a meeting in case learners cannot agree on one. Divide each topic into several points for discussion, for instance:
   - deciding on a new company headquarters (location, design, facilities);
   - brainstorming a new product (type, development procedures, sales points);
   - merging with a competitor (corporate product, corporate image, corporate identity).
2. Writing the exponents you want to present in the **Development** phase on an OHP transparency or flipchart sheet (concealed at first) will save time later.

You will need

- one copy of Worksheet D5.1 per learner;
- one copy of Worksheet D5.2 (cut into 16 cards) per group of three to four learners.

The Activity

Introduction

1. Warm up by brainstorming things that can go wrong in meetings and why; for example: the chairperson / participants arrive late, there is no agenda / no one has read the agenda / no one sticks to the agenda; the chairperson / one participant dominates the meeting; the meeting is too long / short; decisions made at the meeting are not followed up.
2. Working in pairs, learners list things the chairperson should do *during* the meeting. Collect the results on the side of the board.
3. Write a range of suitable exponents on the board in random order (see **Language** for suggestions). Still in pairs, learners try to match them to the class list of things a chairperson should do.
4. Hand out one copy of Worksheet D5.1 to each learner and ask them to write in exponents as appropriate. Check their decisions.

Development

1. Ask learners to suggest a topic for a meeting or choose one from a list (see **Before the lesson** for some ideas).
2. Learners choose a chairperson for the meeting.
3. Shuffle the role cards (Worksheet D5.2) and deal them out so that everyone except the chairperson has three or four.
4. The chairperson now draws up an agenda for the meeting and writes it on the board, while the participants check that they have suitable exponents for their role cards. They may need to look back at their notes for the previous activity (**D4: Taking part in meetings**). Remind the chairperson that their role is not so much to speak themselves as to ensure that all the other participants give their views.

Production

1. The chairperson opens the meeting, goes through the agenda and asks someone to start the discussion.
2. The other learners contribute to the discussion according to the instructions on their role cards, regardless of their real views. They turn over the relevant card as they carry out each instruction.

   The chairperson is responsible for keeping the discussion going until the agenda has been dealt with and all the cards have been used. Ask the participants to note which of the expressions on Worksheet D5.1 the chairperson actually uses. They could give feedback on this following the meeting, along with an appraisal of the chairperson's overall performance.

Further idea

Learners discuss and draw up a list of tips for a chairperson.

Notes

Self-assessment

Meetings should ideally be videoed so that learners can watch and assess their own performance. If this is not possible, an audio recording can also be very helpful.

Using this activity at different levels

Lower-level learners will probably find the **Production** phase of this activity easier if they have a 'dry run' discussion of the topic before starting the meeting proper.

Advanced learners can be asked to brainstorm further exponents and make more challenging interventions in the meeting, such as persisting in their point of view, expressing doubt, supporting a fellow participant or amending the chairperson's summary.

One-to-one lessons

This activity requires a minimum of three participants. Individual learners can however usefully work through the **Introduction** phase with you as a partner.

Follow-up

The **Production** phase of this activity can be reused at intervals, with a different topic and chairperson on each occasion.

Whenever he is bored, Kyle Anderson drifts off into a fantasy world

THE WORKSHEETS

THE WORKSHEETS

THE WORKSHEETS

Mind maps

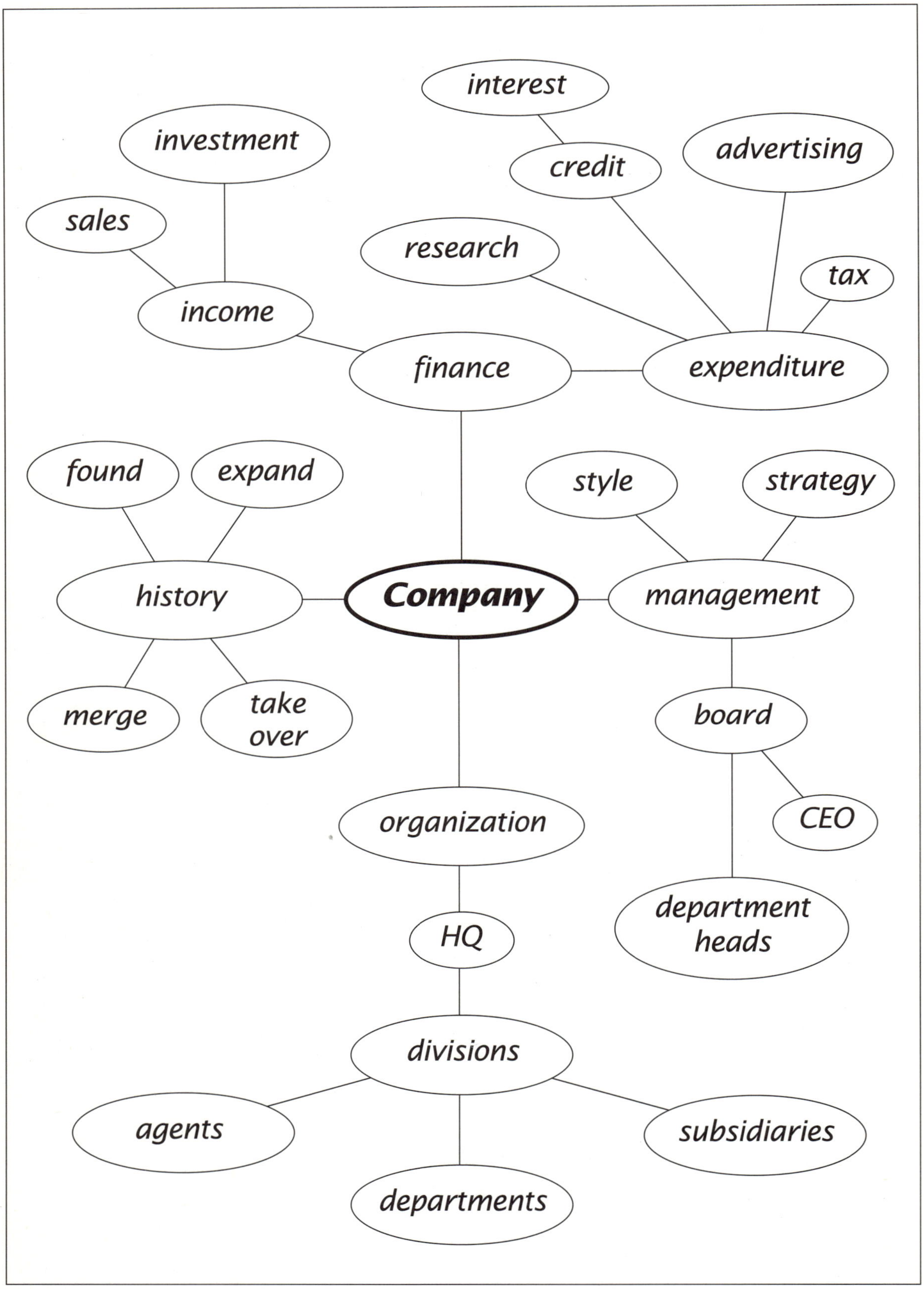
interest
investment
credit
advertising
sales
research
tax
income
finance
expenditure
found
expand
style
strategy
history
Company
management
merge
take over
board
organization
CEO
HQ
department heads
divisions
agents
subsidiaries
departments

Mind maps

after-sales service
customer
delivery
storage
warehouse
R & D
design
factory
production
market research
purchasing
Product
range
raw materials
marketing
advertising
sales
invoice
brochure
promotion
price
bad debt
price list
discount

Word families

ORGANIZE	*organizer*	*organized, disorganized*	*organization*	*organizational, organizationally*									

Word families

Word partnerships

		headquarters
	company	

1. Our company headquarters is in ...

Word partnerships

Starter phrases

I'd like to	*make an appointment with …*

Starter phrases

	A	B	C	D
1				
2				
3				
4				
5				

	A	B	C	D
1				
2				
3				
4				
5				

Brochures

Allianz AG is Europe's leading insurance group, with a current premium income of over DM55 billion per annum. Allianz employs more than 60,000 staff worldwide, supported by a further 180,000 agents and representatives.

Allianz's indemnity and accident insurance division is headed by Allianz Versicherungs-AG and includes Bayerische Versicherungsbank AG (Munich), Frankfurter Versicherungs-AG (Frankfurt am Main) and Allianz Allgemeine Rechtsschutzversicherungs-AG (Munich), together with several smaller subsidiaries. Our activity in this area involves virtually all aspects of casualty and acccident insurance and serves the full spectrum of income groups and types of business.

Annual domestic premium income for our property insurance division currently stands at DM12 billion, with more than 30 million insurance contracts covering some 40 million risks. The division deals with more than three million claims annually. Allianz is Germany's largest insurer of both private and industrial property, and leads the world in technical insurance.

Allianz Lebensversicherungs-AG is responsible for the group's life business in Germany. With a domestic market share of approximately 12.5%, Allianz is by far the largest German life assurer, handling some eight million policies at a total insured sum well in excess of DM200 billion.

Central to the needs of our clients and therefore a key element in Allianz Leben's product range is the "with profits" life assurance policy. Two-thirds of our clients now choose this type of policy with the option of an annual earnings-linked adjustment of premium and performance. Allianz Leben has a curent premium income of DM10 billion and capital reserves of over DM80 billion. (1992)

Manuals

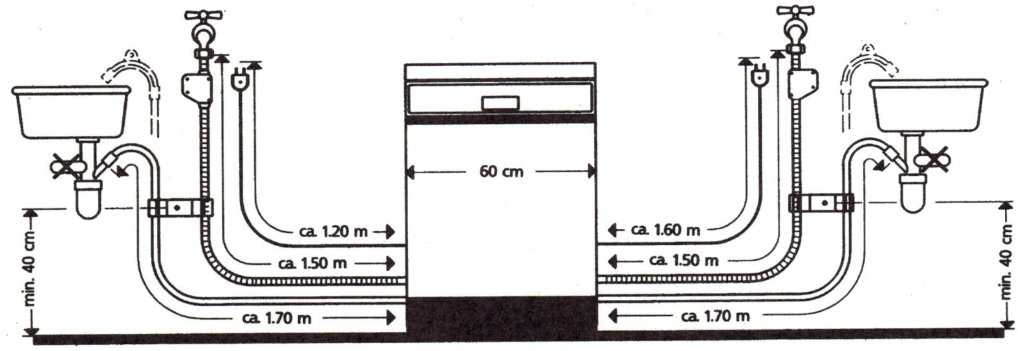

This dishwasher is delivered ready for installation; it has a power cable with plug, inlet water hose and drainage hose. It can be put into operation without special installation requirements if there is an earthed electricity point (installed by a qualified electrician), a water inlet and a drainage connection where the appliance is to be situated (see Figure ①).

Build-under and integratable models are delivered without a worktop. Their height is, therefore, only 82 cm and they should be installed under a continuous work surface which covers the appliance completely. All other dimensions are the same as on the free-standing model.

Data regarding electrical connection and fuse requirements can be found on the rating label on the right-hand side of the door.

Connection of the appliance should be made only to a properly installed, earthed plug and/or socket. The relevant regulations of the local electricity authority should be observed.

The valve casing on the water-stop hose contains electrically-controlled components. It should not, therefore, be submersed in water. If the housing becomes damaged, the plug must be removed from the socket.

(from the installation instructions for "**Juno**" dishwashers)

Green mains telltale ②
This lamp comes on when the appliance is properly connected to the mains and switched on.
• If the lamp goes out, first check whether the bulb has blown. The bulb has blown if the yellow Superfrost lamp comes on when the Superfrost button is pressed. If this lamp also fails to come on, check that:
• the appliance is switched on
• the fuse in the supply circuit is intact.
If you detect a fault that you cannot repair yourself, call in a qualified electrician.

Red warning lamp ①
This lamp comes on when the temperature inside the freezer compartment is too high.
• This is always the case when the freezer has just been switched on.
• High temperatures may also occur when fairly large quantities of fresh food are placed inside for deep-freezing.
• The lamp may come on when the temperature adjusting knob is moved from a higher to a much lower setting.
If none of the above situations applies, the freezer is still in proper working order. The lamp will go out as soon as the correct temperature has been reached inside the freezer.
If the red warning lamp comes on during normal operation, check that **the appliance door is fully closed and that there was no lengthy power failure immediately before.**
If neither of these circumstances applies, please contact the nearest service point immediately.
• Always quote the complete type designation, spare parts index and appliance number. The type plate is located on the left inside panel next to the last but one drawer.

(from the operating instructions for **Liebherr** freezers)

Robinson & Weeks

Head Office
26-28 Nelson Way
Hemel Hempstead
Hertfordshire HP9 4TZ
Tel. 0442 – 66593
Fax. 0442 – 666603

The Sales Manager
Holz-Möbel Küchle
Mollenbach-Strasse 128
71229 Leonberg
Germany

February 23rd

Our ref: RF/pd

Dear Sir or Madam,

We are a major retail organization, specializing in furniture and household equipment for the British market.

On a recent visit to Germany, we were interested to see some examples of your products and were impressed by their design and quality. We would be grateful if you could send us your catalogue and current price list at your earliest convenience, together with details of your delivery service and terms of payment.

Perhaps you could also let us know what discount you would be able to offer on large orders.

We look forward to hearing from you shortly.

Yours faithfully,

V. Wallace

p.p.

Richard Foley
Chief Buyer

Holz-Möbel Küchle

Mollenbach-Straße 128 • Tel. (07152) 2 02 71
71229 Leonberg • Fax. (07152) 2 12 70

Robinson & Weeks
Head Office
28 Nelson Way
Hemel Hempstead
Hertfordshire HP9 4TZ
GB

02.03.

Dear Mr ____________________,

Thank you for _____________________ of __________________.

We are pleased to send you copies of ___________________________________

and ________________________________.

We would be able to offer you a ______________________ of _____% on all

orders with a value of DM ___________ or more.

Please also find enclosed full details of _________________________________

and ______________________________________.

If you require any further _________________________, please do not hesitate to contact us.

We ______________________________ receiving your order.

___________ sincerely,

B. Schwarz-Angott

Bettina Schwarz-Angott
Sales Manager

Advertisements

SECRETARY

£15,500 pa

Leading insurance company requires experienced secretary for manager of industrial department. Candidates should be confident, self-motivated and well-organized. Good keyboard skills are essential. Knowledge of German and/or French would be an advantage. Some travel. Responsibilities will include organizing sales presentations, seminars and arrangements for overseas visitors.

Apply with full CV and photo to the Personnel Officer, Kent Metropolitan plc, 99 Regent Road, London SE4A 9DB. Tel. 071 - 622 - 1005.

DRIVER

required for senior manager. Must have clean licence. Punctuality essential. Mechanical knowledge desirable. Uniform supplied.

Call Job Search on 079 - 212653.

SALES MANAGER

£32K + car + commission

Based in central Bristol, WMC is a fast-growing supplier of top quality photographic equipment to the domestic and European markets.

We are now looking for a professional with at least three years' experience of sales management to head our sales division. The successful applicant will have an excellent sales track record and a good knowledge of the photographic industry. He or she will also have the ability to build up, lead and motivate a dynamic sales team.

If you would like further details of this challenging opportunity, please write with CV in complete confidence to:

Stephen Martell, WMC Ltd, 19 Park Hill, Bristol BS6 2GD.

PUBLIC RELATIONS OFFICER

Salary c. £ 14,500 pa

Forward-looking retail organization requires ambitious graduate with interest in PR and design. The position involves representing the company to the public and editing our in-house newsletter. The PRO is also responsible for supervising corporate hospitality activities.

Among other qualifications, the ideal candidate will have excellent writing and wordprocessing skills. He or she will be imaginative, personable and a good organizer. Knowledge of business procedures is not essential but would be an advantage.

For application form please contact Jill Weathersby on 071 - 992 - 4042. (Closing date May 17th.)

Advertisements

Position	
Salary & benefits	
Company self-portrait	
Job description	
Qualifications	
Experience	
Personal qualities	

Organigrams

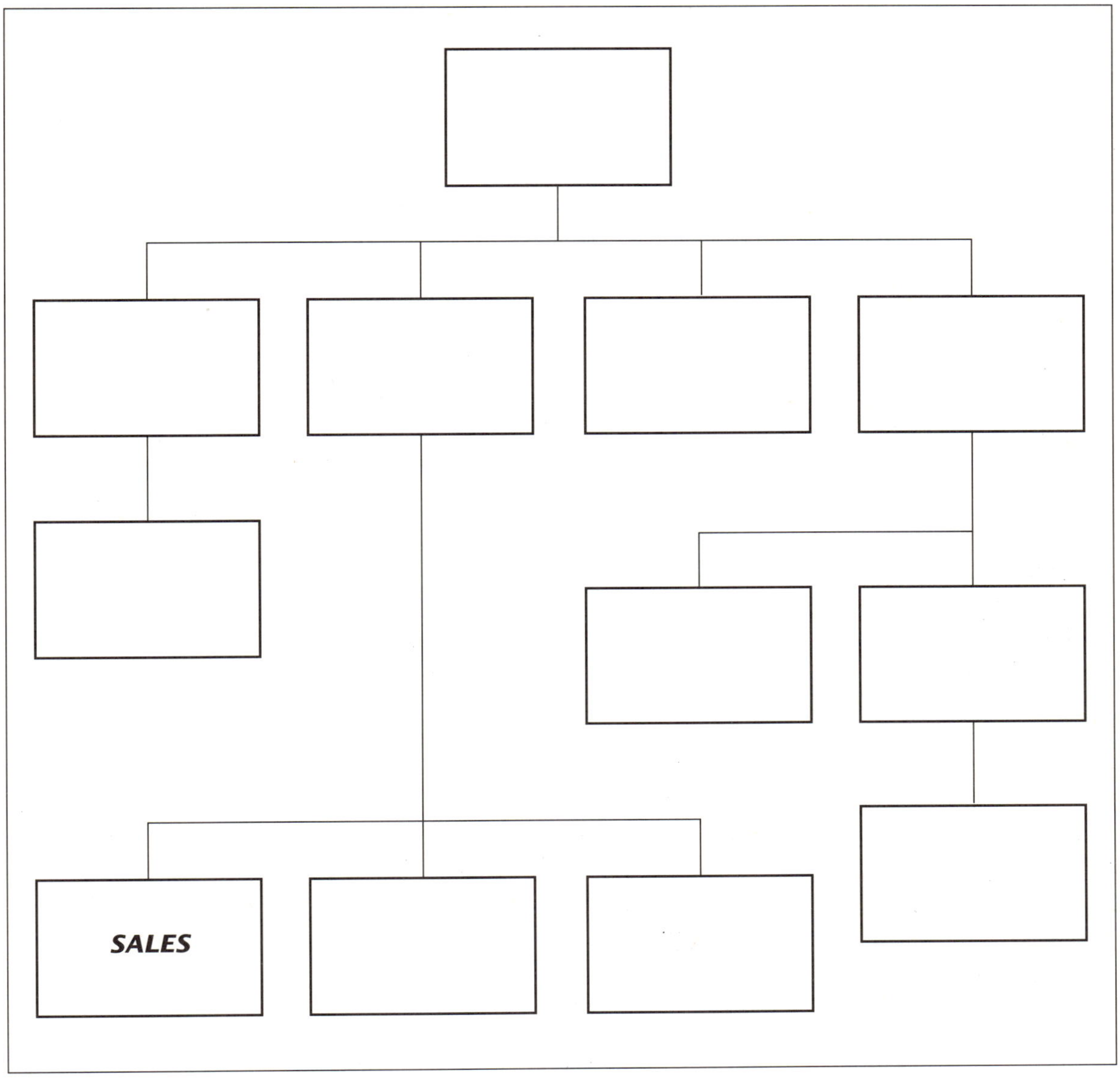

"Well, starting at the top, there's the CEO and the directors. There's the marketing director, for instance - she's in charge of sales and advertising - and the personnel director, who's responsible for everything to do with the employees: contracts, salaries, training and so on. Then there's the head of production; the purchasing and factory managers report to him. The factory manager's responsible for the warehouse, too. Who else is there? Oh yes, the chief accountant, who's responsible to the finance director. And PR; that comes under marketing, too."

Organigrams

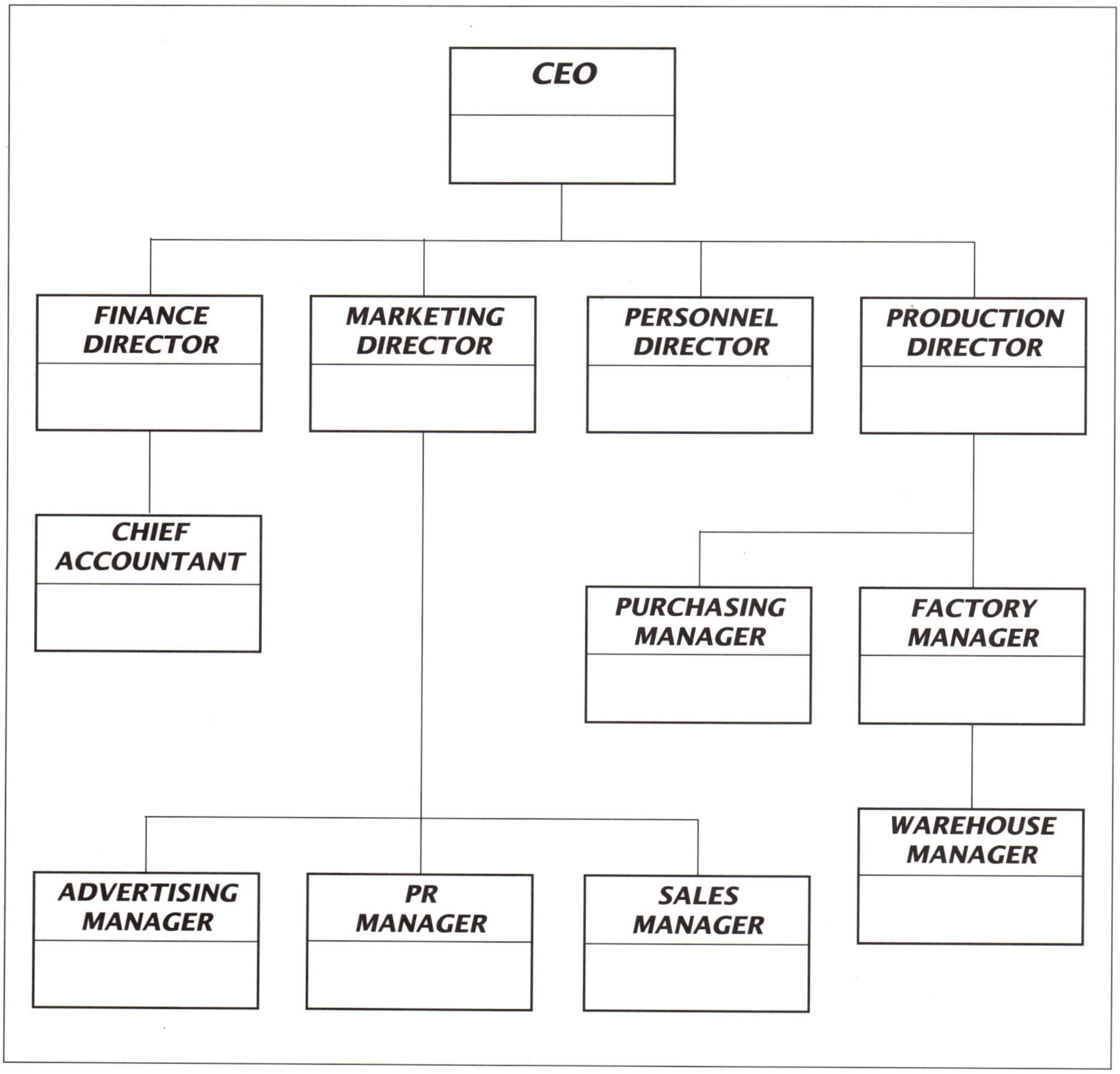

Mrs Hill is responsible for three departments.
The chief accountant is responsible to Mr Forrest.
Mr Peterson reports to Mr Stone but is not in charge of purchasing.
Mr Thomas is responsible for the whole company.
Mr Clark's boss is Mr Peterson.
Mr Browning is the head of the advertising department.

Organigrams

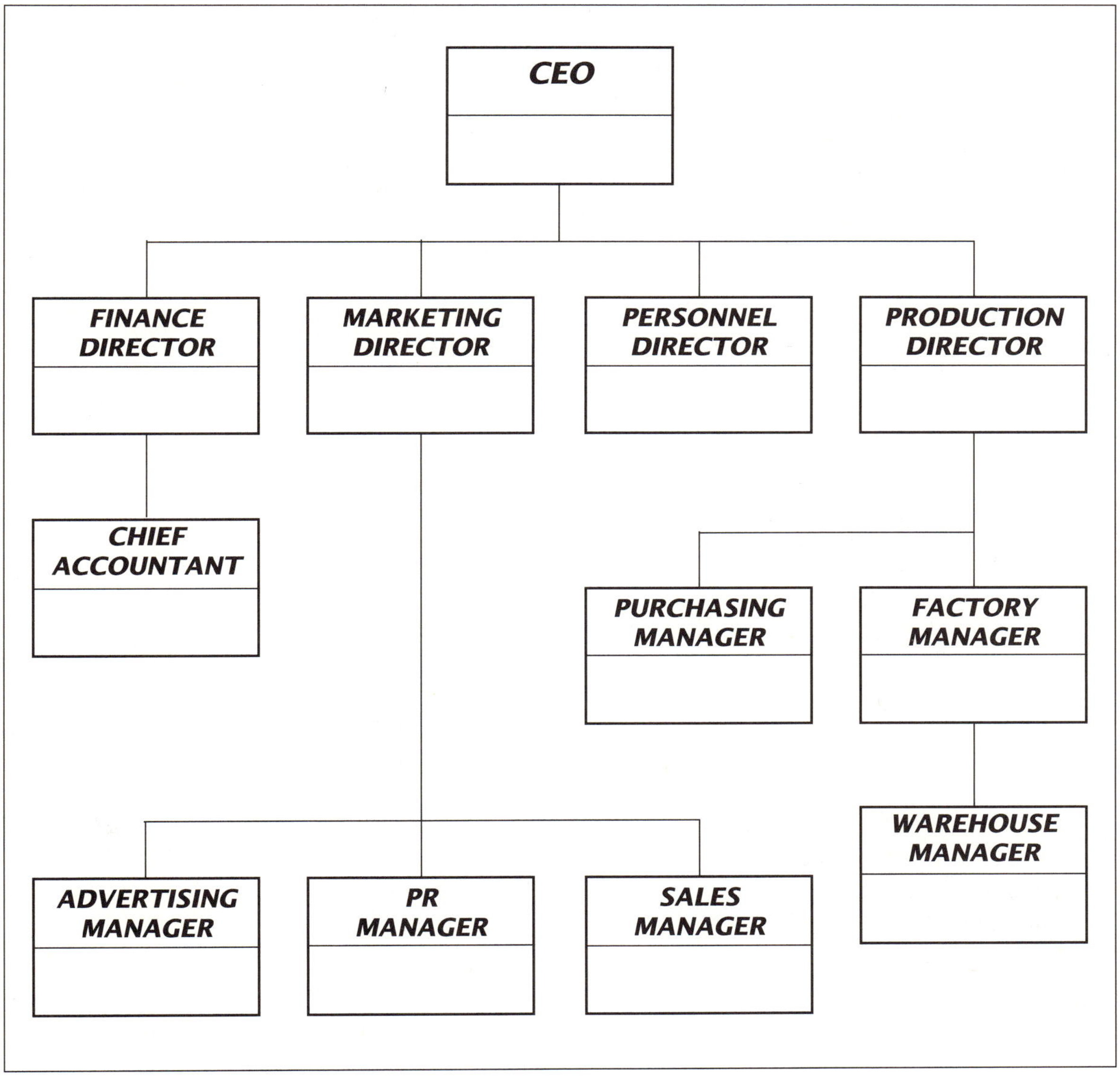

Mr Baker is responsible for the employees.
Two head of department are responsible to Mr Stone.
Ms Alexander is in charge of public relations.
Mr Daniel's boss is Mr Stone.
Mrs Richards reports to Mr Forrest.
The other manager is Mrs Wilkie.

Pie charts

A

1. We export about two-thirds of our total production to France and 25% to other EU countries.

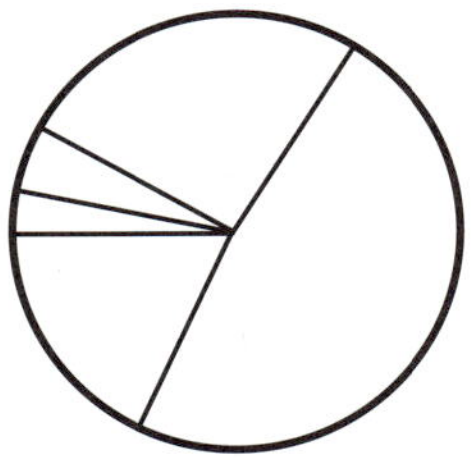

2. Our smallest markets are the US and Japan. We export a little more to the US than we do to Japan.

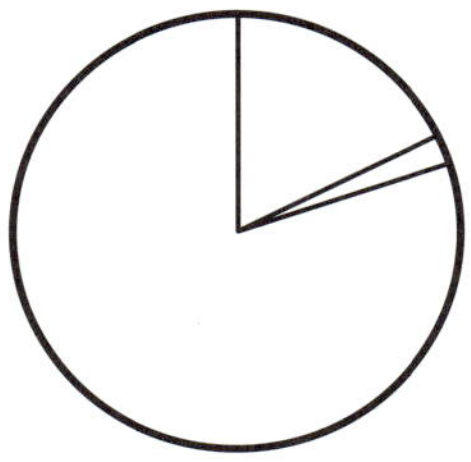

3. Most of our production is for the home market. We export nearly all the rest to Latin America.

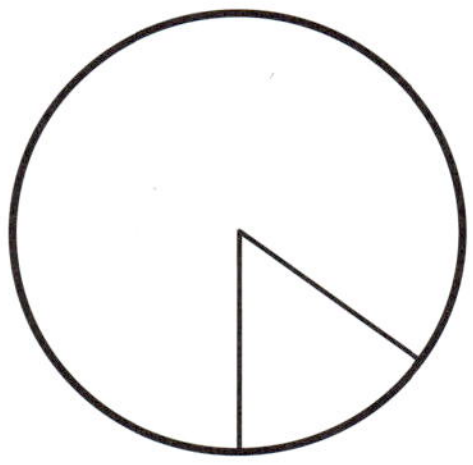

4. Our Chinese market is much bigger than our Indian one.

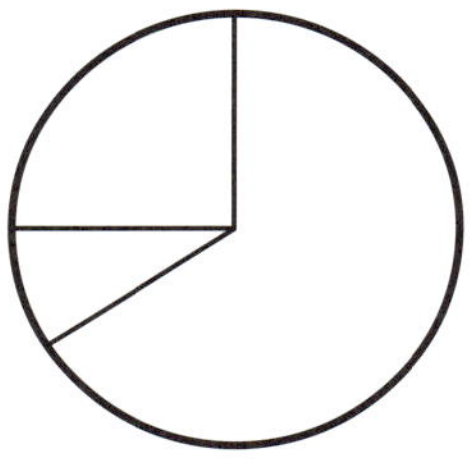

B

Last year we exported nearly three-quarters of our total production. Most of this went to European countries. Germany was our biggest market, with about one third of all sales, and the other EU countries took a further 25%. The rest was divided between the US, Russia and Japan. The US market is still much bigger than the others but for the first time we managed to sell a little more in Russia than in Japan.

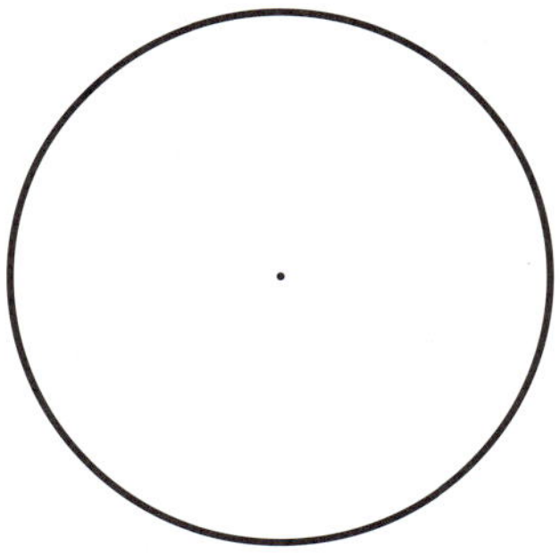

Pie charts

Rawlings Department Store
Sales last year according to department

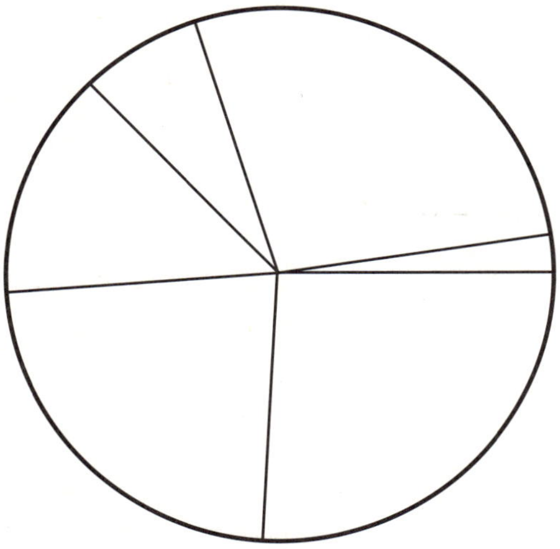

Sampsons Department Store
Sales last year according to department

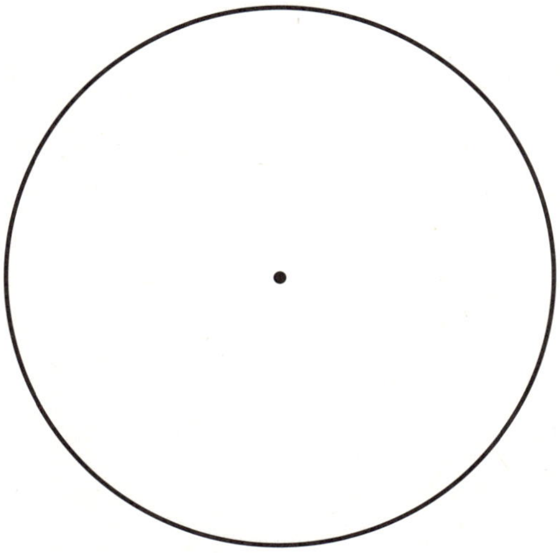

Pie charts

Sampsons Department Store
Sales last year according to department

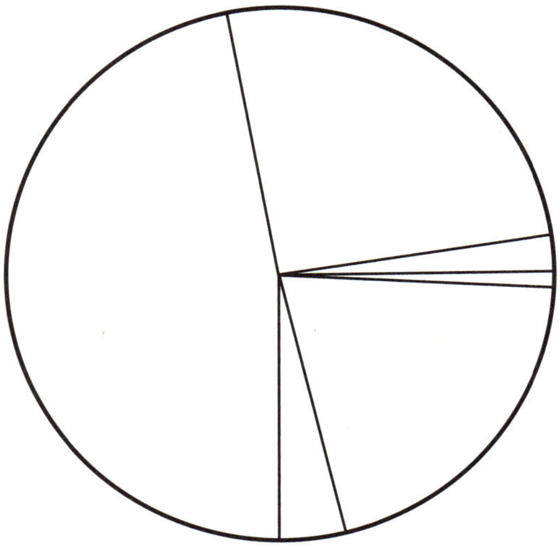

Rawlings Department Store
Sales last year according to department

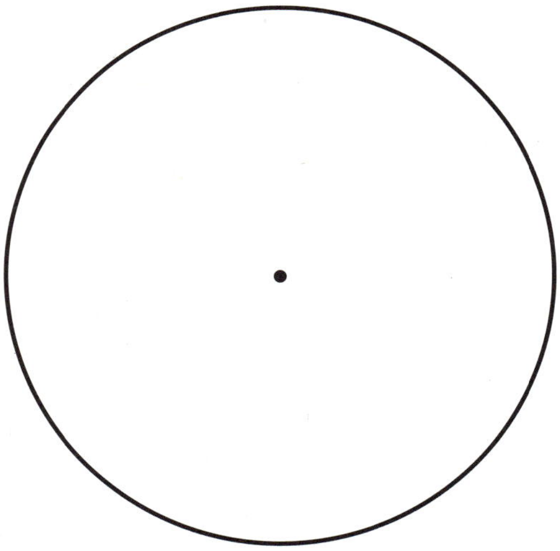

Flow charts

a Next the *Programme* and *Data* symbols appear on the right-hand side of the screen and you have to choose the programme you want to work in.

b When you've finished, you should save your work before you close the document, whether it's a new one or not.

c If you want to work on an existing document you click on the *Data* symbol to call up your files.

d After that you close all the files and programmes.

e But if you want to create a new document you click on the *Programme* symbol and a blank sheet comes up.

f As soon as I've done that, I always copy the document onto a disk in case the system goes down.

g Well, first of all you have to switch the computer and screen on, of course.

h It's best to give the new document a name or reference number straightaway so that it can't get lost.

i After that you have to wait some more and then type your code word in again. I don't know why – I suppose it's got something to do with security.

j After that you can start writing.

k Finally, switch off the screen and the computer.

l Then you have wait for it to warm up and after a while it tells you to type in your personal code word.

m When the list of files comes up on the screen, you select the one you want and start work.

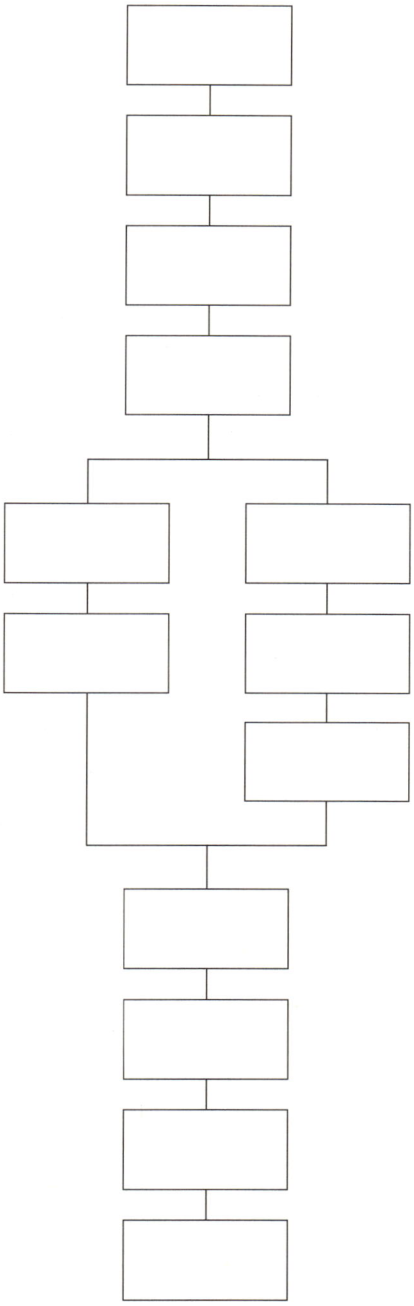

Grids

Companies / *Facilities*	Star Electronics	James Pollock	GT & C	Northern Engineering	York Insurance	Anglo Bank
City centre		●			●	●
Suburbs			●	●		
Industrial estate	●					
Near bus stop / station		●	●		●	●
Employee car park	●	●		●		●
Near shops / restaurants		●			●	●
Canteen	●			●	●	
Creche						
Sports facilities	●					
Air-conditioned offices		●		●		●
Open-plan offices				●		●
Flexitime system	●	●	●	●	●	

Grids

1. ______________ of these companies are near a bus stop or station.

2. ______________ of these companies have got canteens.

3. ______________ Northern Engineering and Anglo Bank have got air-conditioned offices.

4. York Insurance is in the city centre, which means it is near the shops. ____________________________, it hasn't got a car park.

5. Almost ______________ of these companies have got flexitime systems.

6. Star Electronics is on an oldish industrial estate. __________________, they never have difficulty in finding staff.

7. GT & C hasn't got a canteen, ________________ it isn't near any restaurants.

8. Only ______________ of these companies has got sports facilities.

9. ______________ James Pollock nor GT & C have got open-plan offices.

10. ______________ of these companies has got a creche.

some *most* *neither* *one* *both* *although* *none* *all* *on the other hand* *nevertheless*

Grids

Bar charts

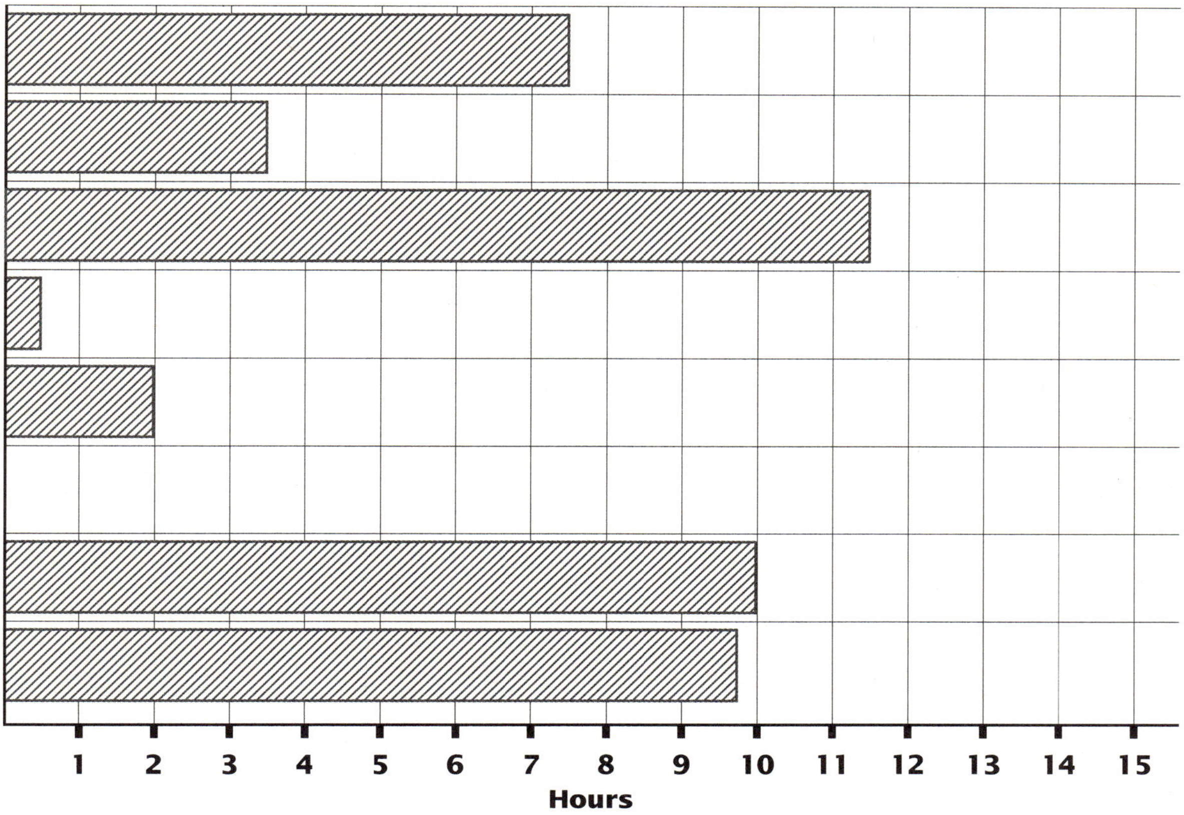

"Last week I spent quite a lot of time on the phone - I should think it was at least one and a half hours per day - and wrote about ten to twelve letters at, say, ten minutes per letter. On Tuesday I had to show some visitors around the company. I usually enjoy doing that but it always takes about three to four hours because you have to go to lunch with them as well. I spent nearly ten hours on a report for my boss and then six and a quarter hours in one meeting and over five in another: awful! I always try to plan the week ahead a bit - I managed to get more or less half an hour for that - and I wanted to read a couple of interesting-looking articles that I've had on my desk for weeks but there just wasn't enough time. And on Wednesday I was on a business trip.

So what's that? Under forty-five hours for the week? Not too bad, really."

Bar charts

Your chart

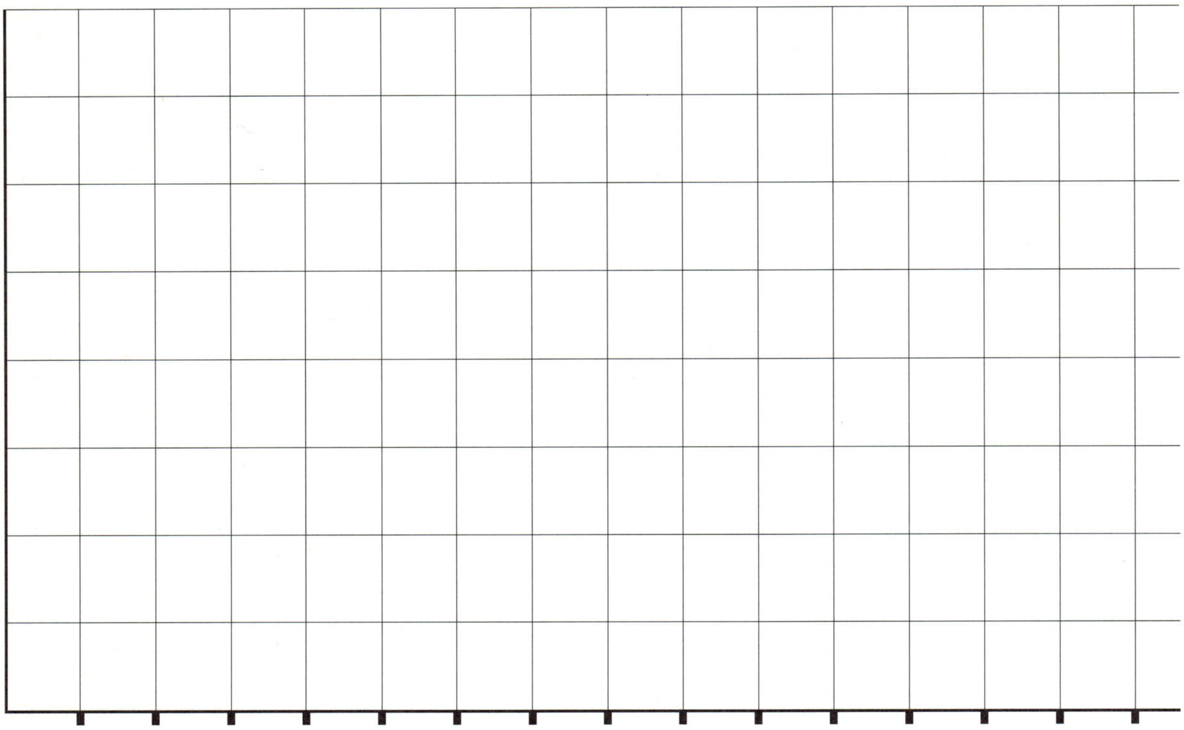

Their chart

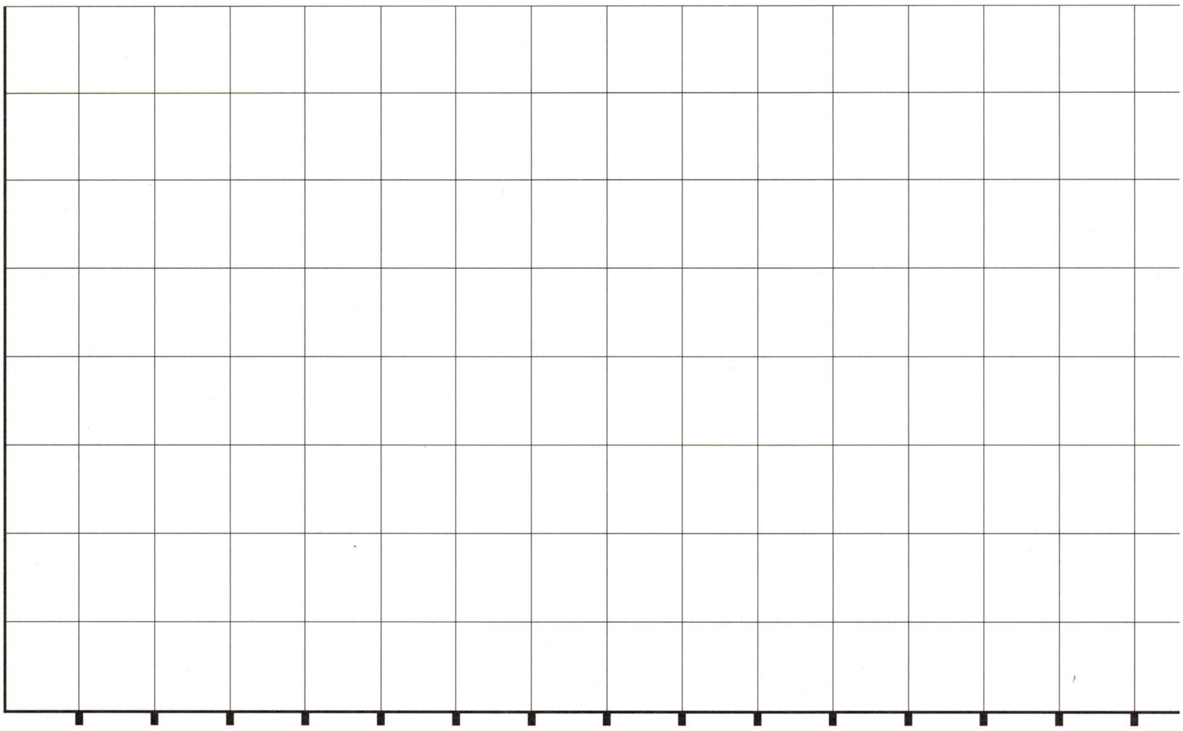

Small talk

Topics	Questions

Structuring a presentation

Greeting / Introducing one-self	
Introducing the subject	
Describing the sequence	
Starting the presentation itself	
Moving on to the next point	
Summarizing	
Concluding	
Thanking / Inviting questions	

Presenting visual information

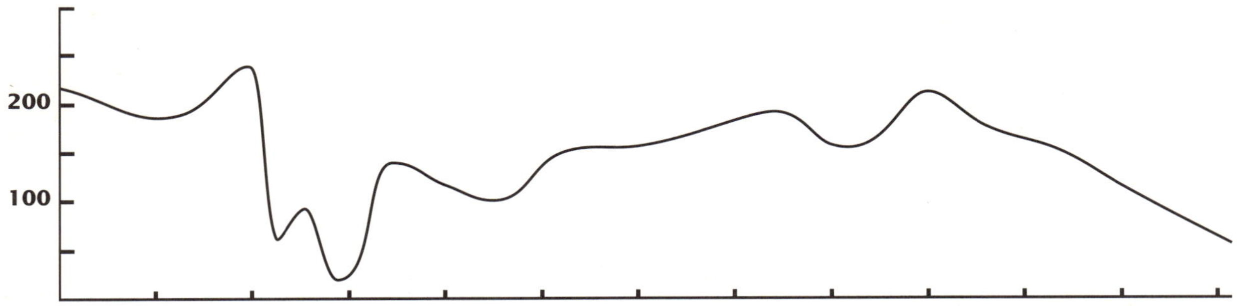

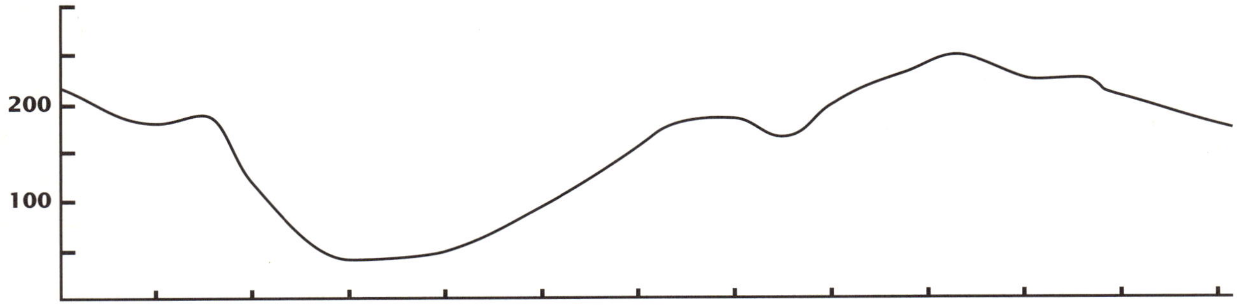

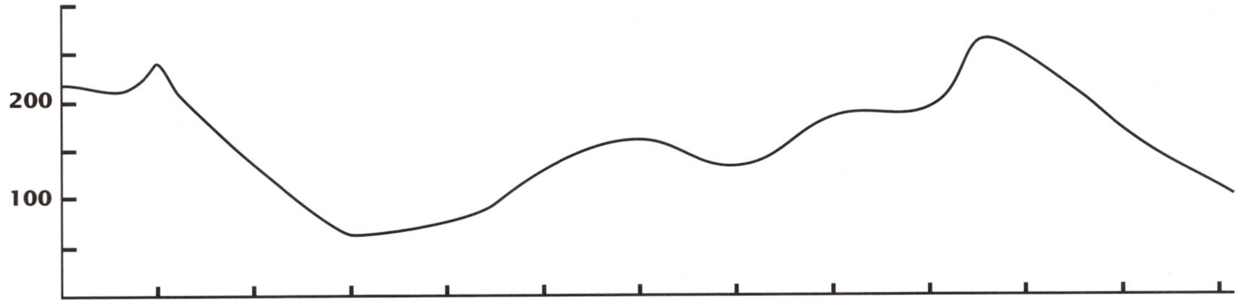

The horizontal axis of the graph shows the months from January to December and the vertical axis shows our total sales in thousands of dollars. As you can see, at the beginning of the year our sales stood at $220,000. They fell throughout January, rose slightly and then fell again sharply in March, reaching their lowest point at the end of the month. From April to June, sales rose steadily, levelling off at around $180,000 in July. After a dip in August, they rose again in September and reached a peak in early October. They then fell slightly, levelled off for a short time in November and fell again gradually to the end of the year.

Presenting visual information

Introducing a visual aid	
Outlining the content	
Focusing	
Emphasizing	
Comparing	
Drawing conclusions	

Taking part in meetings

I'd just like to make two points: firstly, ...	Exactly!
It depends. On the one hand ... on the other hand ...	Can I come in here?
Sorry, could I just finish?	I'm afraid I didn't quite understand.
I'd say ...	Yes, but ...
Yes, that's right.	Sorry, could you repeat that?
With respect, ...	As I see it, ...
There are several issues here: one ...	Could you give us an example?
I'm not sure about that.	In my experience, ...

Taking part in meetings

Giving opinions	
Agreeing	
Disagreeing	
Reacting non-committally	
Asking for clarification	
Interrupting	
Dealing with interruptions	
Gaining time	

Chairing meetings

Opening the meeting	
Outlining the aims of the meeting	
Asking for opinions	
Redirecting the discussion	
Moving on to another point	
Asking for agreement	
Summarizing	
Closing the meeting	

Chairing meetings

Give your opinion	Disagree
Give your opinion	Disagree
Gain time by numbering points	React non-committally
Gain time by numbering points	React non-committally
Agree	Ask for clarification
Agree	Ask for clarification
Agree	Interrupt
Disagree	Interrupt

Book List

Some Klett Business English titles

Resource books for teachers

One to one
P. Wilberg (Klett 937940)

Business Games
J. Mawer (Klett 524080)

General business English courses

Getting Ahead
S. Jones-Macziola and G. White (Klett 502740)

International Business English
L. Jones and R. Alexander (Klett 502750)

Business English
P. Wilberg and M. Lewis (Klett 524030)

Early Business Contacts
N. Brieger and J. Comfort (Klett 538181)

Developing Business Contacts
N. Brieger and J. Comfort (Klett 538190)

Advanced Business Contacts
N. Brieger and J. Comfort (Klett 538260)

Secretarial Contacts
N. Brieger and A. Cornish (Klett 538170)

English for Specific Purposes

Technical Contacts
N. Brieger and J. Comfort (Klett 538340)

English for International Banking and Finance
J. Corbett (Klett 539310)

Finance
N. Brieger and J. Comfort (538240)

Marketing
N. Brieger and J. Comfort (Klett 538220)

Production and Operations
N. Brieger and J. Comfort (Klett 538230)

English in Medicine
E. Glendinning and B. Holmström (Klett 533940)

International Hotel English
D. Adamson (Klett 538730)

International Restaurant English
L. Keane (Klett 538710)

English for Information Systems
S. Hick (Klett 538830)

Language skills for business English

Language Reference for Business English:
Grammar, Functions and Communication Skills
N. Brieger and J. Comfort (Klett 538250)

Business Listening Tasks
P. Hanks and J. Corbett (Klett 533900)

In Print: Reading Business English
R. Revell and S. Sweeney (Klett 534000)

Business skills

Company to Company:
A new approach to business correspondence in English
A. Littlejohn (Klett 533670)

Telephoning in English
J. Naterop and R. Revell (Klett 533931)

Telex English
R. Palstra (Klett 538590)

Business Reports in English
J. Comfort, R. Revell and C. Scott (Klett 533930)

The Language of Meetings
M. Goodale (Klett 524050)

Self-study business materials for German learners

English on Business
G. Lees and T. Thorne (Klett 524000)

Englisch telefonieren
A. Watson-Delestrée (Klett 560955)

Englische Handelskorrespondenz im Griff
R. Armitage-Amato (Klett 560952)

Wirtschaftsenglisch im Griff
J. Flower (Klett 560951)

Englisch Wirtschaft
J-P. Ancelle, T. Shaw, M. Sommers and V. Vermes (Klett 560693)

Dictionaries (English-English with German-English glossary)

Fachwörterbuch Wirtschaft (Klett 517930)
Fachwörterbuch Bank- und Finanzwesen (Klett 517840)
Fachwörterbuch Datenverarbeitung (Klett 517960)
Fachwörterbuch Marketing (Klett 517980)
Fachwörterbuch Medizin (Klett 517990)
Fachwörterbuch Recht (Klett 517950)

Acknowledgements

The authors would particularly like to thank the many learners who have patiently explained their businesses and language needs to them over the years, thereby helping them (hopefully!) to become more effective teachers of Business English.

Thanks are also due to Language Teaching Publications, Hove, G.B. for permission to describe techniques which were first introduced in "Business English" by Peter Wilberg & Michael Lewis (Klett 524030) and form the basis of Activities A3 and A4. The idea for Activity A5 came from a demonstration lesson by Fraser Symon. Shelagh Deller of Pilgrims supplied the original idea for Activity C5 and Michael Tallon and Phil Quirke two of the "Further ideas" in Activity D1.

The publishers would like to thank Herr Werner Lüning, Lübeck, for the right to reproduce the PUNCH cartoons on pp. 14, 26, 44 and 55 and THE NEW YORKER MAGAZINE for the right to reproduce the cartoon on p. 37.

Finally, we are also grateful to Electrolux Hausgeräte GmbH, 35721 Herborn, Germany, and Liebherr Hausgeräte GmbH, 88416 Ochsenhausen, Germany, for permission to print extracts from the instructions for "Juno" dishwashers and Liebherr freezers respectively, and to Allianz AG, Stuttgart, Germany for permission to print the text on Worksheet B1.

Klett

Mobil sein... und Sprachen auftanken mit Super Plus

Selbstlernmaterialien zum Ausbau berufsorientierter Englischkenntnisse

Ganz gleich, ob Kursteilnehmer/-innen Sie um die Empfehlung von ergänzenden Titeln zum Selbstlernen bitten, oder Sie selbst nach Zusatzmaterial für Ihren Unterricht suchen, Super Plus Sprachkurse bieten für jeden die passende Lösung auf dem richtigen Lernniveau:

Englisch Telefonieren
Hörcassette (90') und Buch
ISBN 3-12-560955-0

Wortschatztrainer – Englisch für das Büro
Hörcassette (80') mit Textheft
ISBN 3-12-560492-3

Englische Handelskorrespondenz im Griff
Buch, 160 Seiten, mit Vokabelverzeichnis
ISBN 3-12-560952-6

Wirtschaftsenglisch im Griff
Buch, 104 Seiten, mit Vokabelverzeichnis
ISBN 3-12-560951-8

Englisch Wirtschaft
3 Hörcassetten (180') und Buch
ISBN 3-12-560693-4

English on Business
Lehrbuch, 2 Hörcassetten (175'),
PONS Fachwörterbuch Wirtschaft
ISBN 3-12-524000-X

Für ausführliche Informationen fordern Sie bitte Prospekt P 190687 an,
oder fragen Sie nach in Ihrer Buchhandlung.